casting stones

A Study of Ecclesiastes 3

HEIDI GOEHMANN

ilovemyshepherd

A note on Scripture translations utilized:
Scripture quotations in this study are primarily taken from the
English Standard Version (ESV). When a text is taken from
another translation you will see the following abbreviations:
NIV - New International Version
KJV - King James Version
NASB - New American Standard Bible
HCSB - Holman Christian Standard Bible
NLT - New Living Translation

Please see a full list of references used in the back of this book.

ISBN: 154688260X
ISBN-13: 978-1546882602

Welcome to Casting Stones! Thank you for joining me and opening the pages of this book.

In this study of Ecclesiastes 3, we will explore the seasonal ebb and flow of life and wrestle with the place of dark concepts like hate, uprooting, and tears in our lives. In this journey together, I pray you will see the Light more clearly, even in the darkness. We'll delve deep into topics that rest concretely in Biblical Truth, address some abstract concepts, and identify places in our lives where we have felt uncertain, uncomfortable, or confused as to where God is and what He is doing. We'll study Scripture for its grace and beauty, as well as find applications for our everyday life.

Some questions that will guide us throughout the study include:
What kind of seasons have you seen in your life?
How do we embrace each season as they come to us?
What good is in the mourning?
What is worth dancing about?

Life is good and life is hard. Let's adventure through this life together, around His Word. Before we dive in, a note on how this study is designed. Each week, you can work through the Word in 3 ways:

Daily study readings:
Casting Stones is a nine week study. Each week, you will have the opportunity to work through a segment of Ecclesiastes 3, searching and connecting verses throughout Scripture. The Bread of Life gives us daily Bread in the form of the written Bible. We are not left without counsel. There are five days of study to read each week. You can read it when and where you have the chance. If you miss a day of study in a week, not a big deal! Pick it up again, skip a day, or move to the next week. There is a whole lot of grace here. The goal is to *regularly* be in the Word. It really does make a difference in our daily lives!

Join or facilitate a small group:

Discussing the Word together gives us a firmer grasp on what God is speaking to us personally in that Word, as well as through one another's lives. Connection and community is a deep need in each one of us. God offers us this special gift in His Church and through friendship. Making a plan to discuss the Word over coffee with one friend, three friends, or a dozen others, can not only bring us accountability to be in the Word, but will also add a layer of enrichment to the study that you may not expect.

Scripture Engagement:

Drawing, taking notes, and journaling in the margins of this study book are welcomed and encouraged! Our brains are engaged fully and for a longer period of time, and our hearts are encouraged as well in creative reflection. You will find prayer cards to match each week of study at ilovemyshepherd.com under the Studies Available tab.

You might color each card while you pray. You may jot down prayer requests and post them as a reminder for prayers. You may choose to leave them with notes to encourage someone else, or as decorations on your fridge. The artwork for each engagement tool is a gift to us from other women who have completed this study!

I am so very thankful that you have chosen to invite me in and study the Word with me. I learn so much as I write each study, and especially when I hear from each of you! Do not hesitate to share your thoughts and insights with me by contacting me through the About Me page at ilovemyshepherd.com.

Happy studying, friends!

Love, Heidi ♡

an introduction
to ecclesiastes 3

Ecclesiastes 3:11a
He has made everything beautiful in its time.

week one
An Introduction
to Ecclesiastes 3

Vanity, vanity, meaningless, meaningless
Our friend Ulysses and desperation
To everything there is a season
God's time, my time, and getting them on the same page
Finding ourselves a Solomon

heart verse

I perceived that what God does endures forever...

Ecclesiastes 3:14a

an introduction to ecclesiastes 3

day one
Vanity, vanity, meaningless, meaningless

Oh, Solomon, Solomon! Wouldn't it have been amazing to see this man in all his splendor back in the day? Every time I picture Solomon, I'm reminded of an article I read when I was about 8 years old. The article was the cover story in some kind of major magazine, all about Imelda Marcos, former first lady of the Philippines, who was rumored to have over 3,000 pairs of shoes. I still remember gawking at the pictures in the magazine article. There were glossy images of luxurious clothes and robes. I'm almost positive there were plush seats in the closet, drawers upon drawers of jewelry and handbags, and, of course, the famous rows upon rows of shoes. It was a little girl's dream come true, right there, laid out before me. In Sunday school, I heard the stories of Solomon – his wealth, his wives, his wisdom, his vast kingdom. In my mind, Solomon was the male version of Imelda Marcos and those images still spring to mind to this day!

King Solomon, we know, had lots of stuff. He had lots of wives and children. At one point, he had a solid relationship with God. In 2 Chronicles 1 (and 1 Kings 3), Solomon asks for wisdom and we see him graced by God with so much more. I believe it was the *more* that started to weigh on Solomon. You see, he knew.

Solomon knew that *more* just may be difficult to handle.

Let's open our Bibles and read 2 Chronicles 1:6-12.

The scene changes dramatically by the time we encounter the Solomon in Ecclesiastes, we get the Solomon who has it all and who has tried it all.

Look at what he has to share with us by the time we reach Ecclesiastes 2:9-11:

> *So I became great and surpassed all who were before me in Jerusalem. Also my wisdom remained with me. And whatever my eyes desired I did not keep from them. I kept my heart from no pleasure, for my heart found pleasure in all my toil, and this was my reward for all my toil. Then I considered all that my hands had done and the toil I had expended in doing it, and behold, all was vanity and a striving after wind, and there was nothing to be gained under the sun.*

The above is the ESV translation of Scripture. If you have it available, or are able to jump on the internet, compare this to the NIV translation.

What differences do you notice? Mark anything notable down here.

The thing that jumps out at me the most is in verse 11. Both translations offer an accurate rendering from the original Hebrew language of the Old Testament, nonetheless the NIV is an arrow of truth pointed straight for our hearts. It states Solomon's struggle simply, straightforward, no messing around. Write in the NIV translation of Ecclesiastes 2:11 here:

Everything is meaningless, a chasing...Solomon tells us he wasn't just given it all, but he also *pursued* it all. Through the pages of Ecclesiastes 1 and 2, Solomon shares that he tried fame, fortune, knowledge, work, people, and pleasure. Eventually, Solomon found the truth: None of it satisfies.

In our house, if you mention the book of Ecclesiastes, someone will respond by shouting out, "Meaningless, meaningless, everything is meaningless!" It's an ongoing joke, but also a good reminder of a reality written all over the pages of Ecclesiastes in Solomon's wisdom-filled, heart-poured-out ink:

Without God, everything is meaningless. With God, every single thing has purpose and meaning.

The good, the hard, the gathering of stones, the casting away of stones, every bit of this life is meaningful, purposeful, woven with His grace and significance.

I'm excited to spend the coming weeks with you all. We will glean from Solomon's experiences, discover the poetic heart of our God, and allow Him to loosen and stretch our hearts for His plans and purposes.

This week we will tackle a brief introduction to all things Ecclesiastes by focusing on some commentary and background. We will also hone in on verse 1 of chapter 3 to discover more about God's timing, a message central to all of Ecclesiastes 3.

Hope to see you tomorrow, friends!
Until then, remember this..."Meaningful, meaningful, everything is meaningful!"

Exploration

If you could have more of something in your closet, what would it be?

Nice shoes

If you had been in Solomon's place, what would you have requested from God?

What do you remember of the life of Solomon from Sunday school, reading the Bible, or general knowledge?

- Wisdom (Baby & 2 women)
- parents → David & Bathsheba
- Queen of Sheba

Which components listed by Solomon tend to leave you feeling like life is meaningless – fame, fortune, knowledge, work, people, and pleasure? Tell us why you picked that one.

an introduction
to ecclesiastes 3

day two
Our friend Ulysses and desperation

For a while, there was a popular song on Christian radio that I was just not a fan of. I tried. I really did. I tend to be pretty flexible about types of music I enjoy. I don't have really critical opinions about lyrics. I try to put the best perspective on each artist's work. But every time this song came on, it grated on my nerves and I had to turn the station.

It sounds harsh and critical, so I'm not even going to tell you the name of the song, but the chorus used a repetition of a single phrase, proclaiming that the artist was overwhelmed by God's universe, by His mercy, by His you-fill-in-the-blank.

This song came on during a Saturday afternoon drive. I turned to Dave and said, "I figured it out. I don't want to be overwhelmed. That song may work for some people, but life already feels pretty overwhelming to me most days, and I don't want to be overwhelmed by anything or anyone else. And I'm not sure that's even a good character description of God." I felt pretty solid about my revelation, like wisdom had been expounded to bless the listening ear.

Dave, who had limited previous interest in my struggle with the song, fully supported my contemplations, as a good and caring husband, with a "Hmmmm…that's good you figured it out. So, about that hockey game…" ;)

You may feel like Dave, a little disinterested in Heidi's rant about a random song, but I think Solomon might cozy up to the table for a cup of coffee and a contemplative discussion. Let's see what he has to say in relation to the concept of an overwhelming God, by reading through Ecclesiastes 2:20-23.

Solomon was clearly overwhelmed. He tells us his *"heart despaired over all the toil."* The toil of life can get to us. It's completely normal and in the coming days we'll talk about how it is often "seasonal."

But to some degree, the struggle and the toil of life just is. It always will be. It will not go away. We can let the anxiety build and become overwhelmed. We can experience depression and we certainly need to seek help in lifting us from the darkness, but I don't believe Solomon was dealing with clinical chemical-imbalance depression.

Solomon was dealing with realization.

He discovered that life is struggle. Period. And that in itself is overwhelming. Many of us can relate.

As we become adults, we discover a new weight to life. This weight and its burdens become very real and even crushing as we form more and deeper relationships, take on families, and step closer to mortality. We have all joy in Christ, and still wonder how in the world we missed how difficult it all was the first 21 years of our life.

Luther's take on this was so interesting to me and so exceptionally put, that I had to share it:

"Consider the labors of Hercules, the monsters whom Ulysses (Odysseus) and others had to overcome, the bear, the lion, and the Goliath with whom David had to contend. Any who are ignorant of this art will eventually grow weary." (Pelikan, 1972, pg. 5)

You see, when we are ignorant of the struggle of life, we collapse when we are faced with it. And often times the struggle is a daily realization.

Children die, captive to poverty and malnutrition; slavery is still alive and well in our world; miscarriages and cancer steal loved ones from us. The struggle is real, even on good and wonderful mountaintop days. We are left realizing that the grass does, in fact, wither and flowers do, in fact, fade. Life itself is a chasing after the wind where no legacy we strive for, or ambition we attempt, is enough to leave a true mark.

But again, in Christ our perspective changes. The struggle isn't less, but we can sit in it, live it, watch it swirl around us and not be overwhelmed. The struggle is where we can share the message and see His grace and mercy and salvation. We can live life and live it to the full, not weighed down but lifted up in Him.

Write the following verses out as active reminders of the meaning God gives us in this life through its imperfection.

2 Corinthians 12:9

John 10:10

Thank you, Father! Thank you for struggle and mercy and daily provision. Thank you for Your gentle love and Your perfect justice. To You, O Lord, we lift up our days, our families, and our work. Tend to us with Your care and help us to shine You in all we do. In Jesus' precious name, Amen.

Exploration

When in your life did you first become aware that there were struggles?

When you were young, what person or people helped you to process the difficult things in the world around you?

Can you think of any moments that you were able to help someone else through a struggle (large or small!)?

an introduction to ecclesiastes 3

day three
To everything there is a season

I love seasonal living. Yes, I could live without them, but for the brief autumn that we lived in Haiti, I eagerly scanned my Facebook newsfeed for any pictures of people picking apples, or sitting around plump orange pumpkins, or drinking their pumpkin spice lattes to their hearts' content. Don't get me wrong, living on an island with the beach nearby had its benefits, but my internal clock is firmly set to mark the changing of each season.

In fact, I believe that all of our clocks are set to mark seasons.

Open your Bibles to read Ecclesiastes 3:1, to begin today's study. Write it in the margin if that's helpful for you.

Our internal clock isn't just about falling leaves or spring's crocuses. Our clock is set by a Creator who knit us in the womb and wove our DNA into place. He set our hearts on eternity in Him (Ecc. 3:11) and created us for the seasons of life.

Our present season may look like a new job, or a move, or the same old same old. Our present season may welcome a new baby or an empty nest. It may herald in marital anniversary bliss or marriage darkness. It may have us caring for children, or caring for parents, or both. It may find us surrounded by people and affection, or it may find us feeling very much alone.

Commentator Matthew Henry says it so well:

"The day will give place to the night and the night again to the day. Is it summer? It will be winter. Is it winter? Stay awhile, and it will be summer. Every purpose has a time. The clearest sky will be clouded…joy succeeds sorrow; and the most clouded sky will clear up."

It isn't about analyzing our present season, although that is valuable. It is about knowing that God does, in fact, have a time for us, in all things.

The big things –
    A season for independence
    A season to get married
    A season of fun and exhaustion with little ones
    A season for career "success"
    A season for a new job
    A season of good health
    A season of health struggles
    A season of watching children take wing
    A season of retirement
    A season of death

And the little things –
    A season for vacation
    A season of busyness
    A season of tightening the belt of finances
    A season of plenty
    A season of coffee, coffee, and more coffee
    A season of grumbling
    A season of romance

Recognizing that God weaves us in and out of seasons in our lives, we can stand through the dark stuff knowing that this too shall pass. And when we are waiting desperately for something, we can be assured that our season for that may just be around the corner.

It gives us a little bit of patience and a whole lot of assurance that our God holds our days in His hands. The same God who sends the sun over the horizon and causes it to set at dusk, the God who makes the snow fall and the flowers spring up a few months later, holds our lives and our plans close to His heart.

Look up the words of the Psalmist in Psalm 31:15-19.

Now go back to the lists and circle any of the seasons listed that you have found yourself in at one time or another. Feel free to add any other seasons that come to mind as well.

What season are you in currently? Is it a joyous time, or a season of struggle? Is it a season of normal and average (which is a blessing sometimes!) or surprise and excitement?

To everything there is a season. Whatever the season, embrace it as a time to know a little more of the One who creates and sustains and brings us to the next season. May your seasons ever be a further revealing of His work in your life.

Exploration
What is your favorite season (winter, spring, summer, or fall) and why?

Use this space to reflect on your current season of life (see the questions within today's study if you need a little direction).

In what ways have you seen God work in your seasons?

day four
God's time, my time,
and getting them on the same page

To begin today, please write out Ecclesiastes 3:1 –

Writing is a good way to help things stick to our brains and is a good way to get us all "on the same page" to work through our study. Thanks for doing that!

Ecclesiastes 3:1 is the introduction for the poetic form found in Ecclesiastes 3:2-8, which will be the bulk of our study. Take a moment and underline in your Bible every instance of the word "time" in the entirety of Ecclesiastes 3:1-8.

How many instances did you get? I got 28 using the ESV translation. But no matter what number you got, clearly a major message of this passage is time: God's time, our experience of time, and where the two meet.

Let's firm up what we know about God's time. You don't have to go very far to get a good overview. Let's look at verses from the end of Ecclesiastes 3, as well as a couple from other parts of Scripture. Look up the following verses and jot down what you learn about time from each selection.

Ecclesiastes 3:11, 14

2 Peter 3:8-10

Acts 1:6-8

Here are some touch points we learn from these verses:
- God's time is indeed different from our own and it is something that He reveals to us as He sees fit.

- God makes everything beautiful in time. (Thank you, Jesus!)

- The fullness of God's time is written on our hearts. We yearn for Him and His time and our hearts know the way that we experience time is not all there is. Just as we long to know Him, we long to know and understand His time. In this we live in a duality. We seek His timing in our lives, honoring that He knows better and His time is better. We work within time on earth, but we also leave the real work to Him. What does this balance look like? That's a good question for discussion!

- Everything, absolutely everything, happens under God's counsel.

- God is concerned ALWAYS, first and foremost, with the salvation of people. In everything in our lives then, when we consider timing, we can ask ourselves "What is God concerned with here? Where would He have me place my priority?" Salvation is #1 on the list.

- The time of God is very much wrapped up in the character of God. We cannot understand one without the other. For instance, God is merciful and looks for opportunities to show mercy and grace. We see this in His patience, His seeking "of what has been driven away", and His sending of the Holy Spirit in Acts, for Divine guidance and comfort.

We want to believe that we have complete control over our lives. We want to believe that if we just manage our time well, then the ducks will all line up in a successful row. In reality, in having free will we have some control, however, we can only work within God's framework and counsel or we can chose to strive outside of it, which will end up as a constant battle as we wrestle for control, that was never ours to have.

Even Jesus had to work within God's time during His incarnation. In John 7:30 we see this reality. Underline the reference to time in this verse, which you'll find below. If you are interested in a little further study, look at the whole of John 7 in your Scriptures, using the ESV or another translation, and identify any references to time.

> *So they were seeking to arrest him, but no one laid a hand on him, because his hour had not yet come.*

His time had not yet come, but when it did…wow! The earth shook and the curtain ripped open, salvation is come to us, the inner sanctuary forever opened to His children. His time was worth the wait in 33 AD, and I'm positive it's worth the wait now.

Let's step back and hand it to Him in prayer.

Lord, Your time is so much better than my impatience. You know the hours, the days, the minutes of our lives, even the seconds of our lives; and the lives of those we love. Lord, help us look to you always. Help us trust in Your time, in Your seasons, in Your purpose and plans for our lives. We lay whatever concerns we have on our hearts before you. In Jesus' name we pray, Amen.

- Stefani (VBS)
- Michelle Bird (Hubby deploying on early natwk for 12 mo)

Exploration

Is time important to you? Are you a punctual person or do you tend toward being a tad late (or really late)?

What areas of life do you most often like to have control over?

What areas of life do you most often feel like you have very little or no control over?

an introduction to ecclesiastes 3

day five
Finding ourselves a Solomon

My husband, Dave, and I are big fans of the show, *The Middle*. I like the idea that there are other families struggling to get it together, to care for each other and to find meaning in the day, when so many tasks need to be done and life keeps coming at you full force.

Our favorite episodes have to do with the Heck family's experiences in church. On one particular episode the mom, Frankie, was especially energized by a sermon while visiting a friend's church. The message the sermon left with the hearer was that we need to "Get our business done!" Frankie spends an entire episode trying to figure out what her business is and how to get it done. You can imagine why it might be comedic. Clearly, the business the preacher was imploring had to do with the message of Christ, but sometimes it's not all that clear what that looks like in our specific place and time. This trouble can be multiplied when we are a) not in the Word regularly and b) not gathering with His people regularly.

In Ecclesiastes 3:11, Solomon states:
> *I have seen the business that God has given to the children of man to be busy with.*

We all have business in this life – tasks to do, vocations to fulfill. Solomon tells us that He has seen the tasks and the toils of daily life. He has been there and He knows what joy and vexations come from our business. He knows that we have all been given different work. Continue reading in Ecclesiastes 3:12-13.

Solomon encourages the hearer to "do good" and "take pleasure" in his work on earth. A few thousand years later, we would do well to have a person like Solomon in our own life. We need people who will exhort us, people who acknowledge our lives as they are, as well as the meaning God works into them. We need people who will sit with us in the day to day, people who will encourage us through our tasks. We also need those who will help us see God's truth and help us see our lives through the lens of God's truth, rather than our own.

What kind of people do you have around you in your life? Who is wise and shares the way God sees the world with you? Do you have a friend or family member to help with discernment and direction?

Like Frankie Heck, we all know we have some business to do, but figuring out what that is can be the challenge. What would God have us spend our time on? What is our task for the given day, for our families, and for our Kingdom work on earth?

We need people in our lives who will help us sort this out, around the Word of God, with discernment and in prayer. We need our husbands, our sisters, and our churches to help us sort through the stuff of life. We will find a few Solomon's who will help us discern the God-things and the good things, and the good things from God to spend our time on.

We will have an eternal impact, because God is in us. His Spirit reigns in our hearts, and so His legacy is not lost in the midst of our business. Change those diapers, teach that class, love that husband, turn in that paperwork. All of it we know is good, in God.

And when we feel a little lost, take the opportunity to sit across from your Solomon with a cup of coffee or a juice, and seek some discernment.

Gettin' our business done! He will do it, sister. He surely will do His business in us and through us.

Exploration
What does the present "business" of your life look like? What work or effort or service are you involved in during this season?

Whom has God sent you to discern with in this life, now or in the past? Who do you offer insight to, by sharing God's Word and vantage point?

beginnings and endings

Ecclesiastes 3:11a
He has made everything beautiful in its time.

week two
Beginnings and Endings
Ecclesiastes 3:2

Birth and the invisible umbilical cord
At the loss of a friend
Farm livin' or a time to plant
Plucking up is hard to do
Nations, constitutions, and things that pass away

heart verse

*For everything there is a season, and a
time for every matter under heaven:
    a time to be born, and a time to die;
    a time to plant, and a time to pluck up
    what is planted;*
                    Ecclesiastes 3:1-2

beginnings and endings

day one
Birth and the invisible umbilical cord

What is birth?

The question sounds esoteric, like we are sitting in a library with dark, rich wood walls and big cushiony leather seats. There are green Tiffany lamps around us, and we are smoking cigars, sipping Scotch, contemplating life. But it isn't an unreasonable question when you are taking apart a passage of Scripture.

Language is something we sometimes take for granted, but there's a reason why we have our pastors learn Greek and Hebrew. It's important to understand the words we study in Scripture, apart from our own cultural assumptions and interpretations. These words are God's love notes to us, after all. Each word gives us understanding and insight into Who this Great God of ours is, and what He has done and continues to do for us.

So, let's look at some touch points from Scripture about birth, what it is, and why it matters to consider it.

Birth is FROM God.

First, please read through Job 38:28-33. Write down anything in creation that is referenced in the passage. Try to be detailed, even if something is in a grouping, list everything separately.

Who births the frost? Who set the stars in place and designed the constellations? God addresses these hypothetical questions to Job. God's pen takes several chapters in the book of Job to help us understand that birth is always *from* Him. I asked you to be detailed and specific because God is detailed and specific here. He sees stars together in the expanse of His universe, but he also knows every one of their names. He wasn't just there when they were created. He birthed them. Anything that is birthed, He sets it into motion and causes it to be.

Birth TIES US TO God.

Read Psalm 22:10 found below. Underline the verbs in the verse.

> *On you was I cast from my birth,*
> *and from my mother's womb you have been my God.*

Birth ties us to God. He is wrapped up in begetting, delivering, creating, and fathering. It is an intimate part of His work. We cannot know the Creator without understanding that He values birthing new things into being. We were all in fact born. That alone ties us to the Creator of the Universe, like an invisible lifelong umbilical cord, whether we care to admit it or not. Therefore, births themselves remind us that we are intimately connected to something outside of ourselves, that this isn't all there is to life. There is Something, Someone, greater than us.

Casting is not a verb we would normally relate to birth, but it fits nicely in with our study of Ecclesiastes 3! Notice how the Psalmist uses the phrase in Psalm 22, above. Knitters will understand, we are cast on to God from birth, and by birth, He means the womb. We are connected to Him from the beginning of all our beginnings – planned before time, known by our Father in heaven.

Births are the beginning of SOMETHING NEW.
Read Isaiah 43:19 and write the word new, as large as you can manage, in the space below.

This may seem slightly redundant, but it cannot be missed! Births are the beginning of something new, and we are reminded that God is at work. He is constantly doing something new in our lives: always working, always forgiving, always knitting, growing, and stretching us. That also means that births may make us a bit uncomfortable. Small births – a new path, a new plan, a new idea…these bring some level of surprise, discomfort, or unevenness to life. We can feel rather restless in change, wondering what is to come. Remembering that birth is God's work, not the Evil One's, can offer some much needed comfort in unsettling seasons of change.

Go back to the word new that you wrote and around it, write some changes that God has worked in your life. Consider, what newness did He bring from each change? Please share some of your thoughts with us here.

Birth is a gift TO BE PRAISED.
Let's read Psalm 71:6 in our Bibles.

Births are a gift of the presence of God, real and tangible. Maybe because Jesus, himself, was born as incarnate God on this Earth, or because birth is a place where our world meets the sacred so obviously for even a moment, but they are to be praised. When babies utter their first cry, how much of that is a natural praise put up before God for His creation, that guttural crying out, as a brand spanking new little one enters the world. Is it for us or is it for Him? Look at Psalm 71:6 again. Write the last sentence of the verse in the space below:

We praise continually, from before birth and through the ups and downs of daily life. Then, when the clumps of dirt fall on our graves, we can be found praising Him in His very presence, with angels and archangels above.

Today, we lift up our praise to Him who calls us out of darkness into His marvelous light. Thank you, Lord, for the birth of Faith!

Lord, we praise you because we are fearfully and wonderfully made. We thank you for molding and making us, and calling us out into Your light, through the birth and death and resurrection of Your Son, Jesus Christ. Amen!

Exploration
Where were you born? What do you know about the details of your birth?

What is something that is born or birthed that we may not traditionally think of in this way (like an idea or a church)?

When have you experienced something new in life that you weren't very excited about?

day two
At the loss of a friend

I opened my computer to write today's study.

It's something I do almost every morning. As I prepare to write, I'm surrounded by some of my favorite things: my husband (quietly working across from me), my coffee, my computer, and my study Bible. I feel warm and cozy.

I open my Facebook feed to idly post a study update, when I see the post that I knew was coming for months, but feels shocking and sad and unfair all the same.

We lost my dear friend, Melissa, to cancer overnight.

I hate cancer. My children would tell me that we don't use the word hate. But cancer, I hate. It robs children of mothers and fathers and grandparents. It eats up time that was meant to be enjoyed together with those we love. It has no boundaries. It touches all of us in some way. It fear mongers, and leaves us wondering when it will come find us. Disease, of any kind, is of Satan, but just like all the dark things on the path behind us and before us, God redeems that too. He redeems what cancer steals. I'm holding Him to that promise.

Ecclesiastes tells us there is a time to die. We know it, but we avoid it. It seems so morbid to talk about it. It's not tea party talk or baby shower talk. But why do we avoid it with those closest to us? Why do we feel so uncomfortable affirming the truth of death in our own lives? I have two theories. One, it's a little bit scary, and, two, it's just so big.

We may avoid talk of death, but the Bible does not. According to Strong's Hebrew Concordance, there are 839 occurrences of *muth* in Scripture. This is the Hebrew root word for *die* in Ecclesiastes 3. There is a place for the reality of death. As Christians, we get to talk about it and shed light in a dark place with no hope. We have Jesus, and we can offer His message to a world who is avoiding death, misunderstanding death, and fearing death.

If something exists, it is either purposeful and from God, or made purposeful by God.

God gave us death to save us from eternal despair and destruction. Death is a door. A way into God's new beginning. With Jesus we can see this. The scales fall and our eyes are opened to what new things God is doing through death –

Heaven (real and tangible), restored relationships, a different path, a desperate need for something else, for a Savior who loves us…

Death teaches us that eternity matters, and so do we. When things die, there is room for rebirth. Without death things become stagnant. Knowing this, we can appreciate that even the death of little things are purposeful…the death of our spring flowers brings winter rest, the death of one idea births another, the death of an activity brings time for something more.

More than that, the death of things we treasure:
- the death of a loved one gives us a greater depth of desire for God and eternity,
- the death of a job opens the door to a new vocation in our lives,
- the death of a friendship can show us who we are and what we value more clearly.

Read Ecclesiastes 3:1-2 again carefully –

> *For everything there is a season, and a time for every matter under heaven:*
>> *a time to be born, and a time to die;*
>> *a time to plant, and a time to pluck up what is planted;*

"Everything in its time" invites us to have conversations about death. This is good and this is necessary. It sounds morbid, but we can be comfortable with it, because we are comfortable with God's hand on it, in it, and around it.

My life will not be quite the same without Melissa. We gathered around the Word together almost every Wednesday morning for 8 years. Her insights and affection have left a Jesus-shaped imprint on my heart and soul. But I know, without a doubt, that God has a plan. He will make this beautiful. His work in Melissa's death will not be lost. He will use this, and many of us will hear a new Word of Grace as we mourn her loss.

Dear Father, birth what you would birth and let die those things that you would have die. It is all in You. Help us to give it to you, for you hold it already. In Christ's name we pray. Amen.

Exploration

Who have you lost that left an eternal mark on you?

What suggestions can you share for helping those who are grieving?

How has someone helped you through loss and grief?

beginnings and endings

day three
Farm livin' or a time to plant

We live in the corn, or the wheat, or the soybeans. It wasn't something I saw coming in my life. But after being here for more than 12 years, I love the growing fields, especially when the sunrise pops over the horizon. All you can see for a mile is shoots of fresh crop sprung up from the ground, and big bold beautiful colors filling the sky, with tiny red barns dotting the space in between. The contrast is amazing. And the food! We eat crazy fresh food. My beef comes from cows I have met, that lived less than a mile away, abundant produce baskets fill the narthex in the summer, and we have, in fact, owned a cow with friends. This is a fact that surprises even me. Rural life has its benefits.

In these past twelve years I have learned to appreciate farming. I learn something new about the techniques and modern mechanisms of farming every day, but something the people of rural America taught me right away is that
God is a farmer.

All we have comes from Him. We plant with our hands, only by His grace. Crops grow, only with His tender care. The harvest is plentiful or lean depending on the need God sees and His plans for men on earth, with the eternal in mind. God calls his earth good.

In Genesis 2:8, God plants a garden for Adam and Eve to reside in, and after forming man with his very own hands, he uses those hands to make a home for them. Fill in the missing words in this verse below.

And the LORD *God* _____

_____ _____ *in Eden, in the east,*

and there he put the man whom he had formed.

God created and created, but He still planted a garden for His children. Remarkable!

As often as God talks about planting in the traditional farming sense, in the Scriptures, he also talks about planting people.

Look with me at Exodus 15:17-18. This passage is at the end of Moses's song, once God had brought the Israelites through the Red Sea onto dry ground.

Where does it say that God plants the people? *With Him.* Yes! On His holy mountain…not aimlessly, but firmly in His care, in His hands.

Just like the Israelites, we are planted with care in the place where God puts us. We are never apart from His presence. We may worship in sanctuaries, buildings made by human hands, but we are the living stones. We are not just built, or even built up, sister. We are planted, with roots that run as deep as His faithfulness. And, oh man, is He ever faithful.

Jeremiah 17:7-8 is my eldest daughter's confirmation verse. Let's write out these two verses in the space at the top of the next page. It may look like a chunk, but it is beautiful and the work will be worth it, I promise.

Jeremiah 17:7-8...

What doubts do you have currently? What fears? Record any that come to mind below.

We pray for strong roots for our children and wings to fly. He gives them both without fail. He gives them just as graciously to each of us. He will never fail us.

We can understand this idea of God planting us because he has planted His very self in us at our baptisms. We are now that sanctuary that houses His Spirit, Himself. We are planted with God always, and need not fear ever being forsaken.

Sometimes it is a time to plant new ideas, new jobs, new friends, new adventures, new challenges. We can embrace all of it with Him, knowing that He will plant firmly what is supposed to remain, while other things will pass away quickly because they are not in His long term plans.

Deciding on something new? Place it before Him.

Lord, plant me deeply in Your Word and Truth. Plant Your Love and Grace ever deeper in my heart. Thank you for sending Your Spirit to live in us and through me. Help me to be ever mindful that there is no greater gift, that You are in me. Guide my life, Jesus. Pluck me up, plant me where You would have me. Help me to identify what is of You and what is distraction. Help me in the struggle of growth. You, O Lord, You are the Farmer and Gardener of my soul. I trust in You. In Jesus' Name, Amen.

Exploration

What is your favorite crop that comes from the ground and why?

Imagine the Garden of Eden. What does it look like in your mind when you picture it?

What new thing is God planting in your life?

day four
Plucking up is hard to do

Today it's time to dig into some Hebrew. Oh fun!

First, reread the passage we are focusing on this week, Ecclesiastes 3:1-2.

The Hebrew word for pluck up in this passage is *aqar,* which we see in the ESV translation as *pluck up,* or in the NIV translation as *uproot.* Furthermore, the visual image produced by this verb is of digging down deep, digging something up *by the roots.*

Let me tell you a story…
There once was a rosebush. (I know some of you love rosebushes, so I apologize ahead of time for this story.)

We moved into our parsonage when my oldest child was just two years old. Right outside of our back door was this rosebush. Our daughter loved to walk out the back door and try to manhandle the rosebush. To her own sadness, the rosebush did not appreciate the attention. She would inevitably get poked by a thorn and I would end up lamenting the very existence of roses everywhere. We tried to teach her to leave the pretty rosebush alone, to no avail. I had to make a decision, rosebush or parenting angst. Rosebush, it's time for you to go.

And here begins the story of the rosebush that would not die.

I hacked away at that thing, year after year, and it came back. I tried to plant things on top of the roots and it always won, killing whatever I planted and popping back up. I finally uncovered a root as thick as my fist. I had to literally get into the hole and dig the root up from a good 2 feet under. There was a fair show of manliness by my husband's friends in chopping through that root to end the story of the rosebush.

But, oh it was worth the fight! Now things flourish and grow in this spot. I planted lavender and Easter lilies, grass that twirls in snappy spirals, and beautiful purple something or others that are delicate and soft, yet hearty and strong.

The rose bush served its purpose for someone, but our family had a different need.

So it goes with plans and programs, and ways that we do things. They can become fruitless, and when they do, we need to **change plans**, to do something new.

Read through Isaiah 43:16-21 in your Bibles.

He is doing a new thing! Not always, but sometimes.

And He gives us what we need *for* this new thing. List for me some of the things He does to prepare or aid in this new thing, according to the passage in Isaiah.

There is a time to plant and a time to pluck up what has been planted. Some things aren't meant for always, and that's ok.

We can plant all the plans we want, but every single plan still has its time in God. If a plan is outside of His will, and we don't pluck it up, He will dig it up. We can ease this process by listening to Him as He speaks to our hearts. We stay in His Word, we read and grow in Him, and He tenderly digs and tends our souls and hearts and lives and plans.

And we can trust His plans. His are always better anyway.

Exploration

When has God done a new thing in your life that felt a little scary in the beginning? How did you work through the struggle of it?

What Bible verses help you to remember God's character and help you to lean in trust on Him?

beginnings and endings

day five
Nations, constitutions, and things that pass away

We, as people alive on this earth, like to feel secure. It isn't an American thing, it isn't attributed to a specific heritage or culture. I have seen it in nations of poverty and nations of wealth, nations with expanse and nations that are tiny dots on the map, every race, every tribe, every tongue. We like to feel like our feet stand on solid rock, our lifestyle is stable, our loved ones, our economic status, and our way of life tightly secure.

In fact, I think we prop security up like an idol. We place all our trust in things that *appear* that they will not perish, will not pass away. Strong armies, glamorous princes, a well-spoken president, a bolstered reserve. In reality, history teaches us well that all of these will pass away.

In fact, they will not just pass away. They will, in their time, be plucked up.

Let's look at Mark 13:1-8. Please read this passage in your Bibles. Jesus is teaching his disciples and those gathered around Him. (This passage, or at least portions of it, also appear in Matthew 24 and Luke 21, if you'd like to do some cross-referencing.)

Buildings have their time. Governments have their time. Nations have their time.

We live in the end times. The Old Testament believers waited for the fulfillment of the promised Messiah and we, as New Testament believers, await His coming again, when all things will be made new, when our way of life is plucked up by God. Knowing this, knowing what is to come, and that it is all in God's hands, we can rest our security soundly where it belongs, with Christ Jesus.

We can and should pray for our nation, for its place and time in history and ask God to work in and through it, but we do not place our trust in it.

What does all this have to do with our study of Ecclesiastes? Context.

Matthew Henry brings up in his commentary on Ecclesiastes that the language of the Old Testament with uprooting, or plucking up, is almost always in relation to nations.

Read Jeremiah 12:12-15, for an example. This passage references both the plucking up of Judah (the Southern kingdom of the people of Israel), as well as the nations surrounding Israel.

God wanted his people to know that they were a people, chosen for a specific place and time, because He had chosen to bring His Son through them to the world, and thereby His saving Grace to every nation on earth. Every nation. His judgment of every nation, every ruler, every person, in their place and time, is perfected in God's desire for all people to be saved. Thank goodness!

I have no opinions about the current political status of the nation of Israel or America, or any other nation for that matter. What I do care about is that God is secure. God is the solid rock. God is eternal, unshaken, our anchor, and no other.

And so we wake up and we lie down. We live our lives. We pray for our leaders. We pray for our military. We pray for our first responders. We thank and praise God for each and every day He gives us safety, and wealth to be stewards of, and peace in our land.

But trust… trust we put in Him and Him alone.

Our King of Kings, our Prince of Peace. To Him be the glory, forever and ever. Amen.

Exploration

What is your national or cultural heritage? How does this influence you?

In what way can politics or national security be a stumbling block to our faith in God? How can it be a blessing to us?

healing and
firm foundations

Ecclesiastes 3:11a
He has made everything beautiful in its time.

week three
Healing and
Firm Foundations
Ecclesiastes 3:3
A time to kill: Putting the Old Testament in context
The healing touch
A time to break down
A time to build up
Laying foundations one home at a time

heart verse

For everything there is a season, and a time for every matter under heaven:
a time to kill, and a time to heal;
a time to break down, and a time to build up;

Ecclesiastes 3:1,3

day one

A time to kill:
Putting the Old Testament in context

Yikes! Now there's a Bible study title!

Killing is not something we chat about around the dinner table. It's a horrific word that has a hard time rolling off my tongue. I do well in my current cultural context, where war is not my daily reality and I can avoid the homicide report on the 11 o'clock news by going to bed early. (Thank you, Eastern Standard Time.)

The Old Testament makes most of us uncomfortable to some extent. It is full of killing that almost always relates to battle or sacrifices. It can be a hard pill to swallow.

We are commanded "Do not kill" in the 5th commandment. Yet, it's a huge part of our history as the people of God on this earth. How do we reconcile it? The answer may be easy for you, but don't forget your neighbor. It may not be as simple for them and part of the reason that we study and grow and learn in the Scriptures is to bring the Word to those dear ones around us. Most of us don't open the evangelistic message with "You see there were all these killings and sacrifices that lead up to Jesus…"

First, let's explore the Old Testament context. Look up the following two passages and jot down anything you find notable. I added a couple of notes myself as well. It's fun to share our different viewpoints when we read the Word together.

Leviticus 14:24-27 – Killing in <u>sacrifice</u>

Reading the Old Testament ritual can be intense, but keep in mind that the lamb always points to Jesus, the ultimate Sacrifice for all of us.

Judges 3:26-30 – Killing in <u>battle</u>

10,000 people killed. Israel rejoicing. Granted, at the end of this passage we have a glimpse into the seasonal aspects of war, but when you read the Old Testament, these are the stories you cannot help but see.

As New Testament believers we can rejoice that the price is paid. We understand the sacrificial system as a giant red blinking light pointing the way to Jesus.

Ephesians 2:14-16 clarifies this point for us. Read the verses below and circle words that offer the hope of Christ.

For he himself is our peace, who has made us both one and has broken down in his flesh the dividing wall of hostility by abolishing the law of commandments expressed in ordinances, that he might create in himself one new man in place of the two, so making peace, and might reconcile us both to God in one body through the cross, thereby killing the hostility.

We have peace! Our life as Christ-followers looks so much different from the Old Testament that it becomes hard to wrap our heads around the ways of the Old Covenant found there.

Look carefully back at Ephesians 2:16 and underline the last four words.

In the New Testament context, God talks about killing whatever divides us from God. The death toll, the turmoil, the killings of the Old Testament accounts are all necessary for us to understand that **we don't live that way anymore.**

Praise the Lord! Glance back up to the Ephesians 2 passage. Dividing wall, gone. Hostility between us and God, killed. Praise Jesus! All that stuff that kept Israel separated from God, longing for His temple and sacrifices to appease Him, destroyed, and lifted up in the death of Christ Jesus on the cross.

Deuteronomy 32:39 says it so beautifully.

See now that I, even I, am he,
*   and there is no god beside me;*
I kill and I make alive;
*   I wound and I heal;*
*   and there is none that can deliver out of my hand.*

We cannot take God in pieces that we like, that are pretty to the eye, but do not nurture truth in the soul. We may not fully understand Him, but we take Him at His Word, for Who He is. I'm so thankful that I don't live in the context of the Old Testament. But I am also thankful for a God who does things in fullness and gives even killing beauty in His work.

He is in charge, but He is also a God that broke down every wall, killed every bit of hostility within us and between us, for our benefit. Praise Him today for the parts of Him you have yet to quite understand, thanking Him for simply being God.

Exploration

What stories of the Old Testament are harder for you to hear?

~ Abraham & Isaac

Do you ever remember being scared of something in the Bible when you were a child?

~ Stonings

What kinds of hostility have you seen God kill, in your life or in the lives of others?

day two
The healing touch

I am terrified of the stomach flu. We sent our kids to school after homeschooling and the morning I walked out the school doors and left them in their classroom, my heart was heavy, but my mind! All my mind could think about was all the stomach bugs I was setting them up to bring home. (Maybe not my most endearing mom-moment.)

But stomach flus come and go in a house of six with some amount of regularity. Every time we are done with a round, I sit myself down on our couch, exhausted, and fall into contemplation about the body's amazing ability to heal. It really is clearly the work of God. All the white blood cells and helper Ts and other good stuff raging a battle inside each of us. Pushing illness out, keeping some illness at bay, sometimes ravaged and putting up a valiant fight. Fevers and mucus and snot...all have their purpose. It's quite miraculous.

And miraculous is always God at work.

The root of the word for heal in Ecclesiastes 3:3 is *rapha*. Maybe it rings a bell for you. You have probably heard of the name for God, *Jehovah Rapha*. God calls Himself this very name in Exodus 15:22-27. Let's read that from our Bibles.

When you come to the words *Your Healer* in your Bible, I encourage you to underline it. This is the translation of the phrase *Jehovah Rapha*.

Rapha in its various translated forms can mean: *to heal, a physician, purify, to make fresh, to repair.*

In this instance of Scripture, God heals by offering His people fresh water. There are so many theological connections here that my head is spinning, but let's just sit with this for a moment. God offered His people a drink, and just like God often does, He then overflowed their cup, in His own time, with 12 springs and 70 palm trees in an oasis in the desert of life.

Where do you need *rapha*? Where do you need a Savior to meet you in the desert?

What does Psalm 41:4 tells us our primary need of healing is from? SIN

Read this verse for a second time out loud, as a private confession of your need for Christ's healing touch.

Jesus offers us His healing, once and for all, in His blood shed for us. Restoring our lives. Draw a cross in the margin to remind you of His absolute forgiveness for you.

What else in life needs His healing touch? Your examples may be your own, or broader, encompassing life and the world in general.

Often our relationships need healing – relational tears, arguments, words spoken too quickly, drama that leaves us weary.

Often our hearts need healing – whether our wounds are fresh and gaping wide open or we bear scars that have long been closed, like shattered hopes, or dreams that have floated away.

Often the journeying aspects of life need healing – we are tired, we have world weary feet, we need rest for our souls.

I love the stories of Jesus healing in the New Testament. They so often have a touch of the deeply personal. My very favorite is found in Matthew 8:14-17. Please read that passage in your Bible.

He touched her hand…
A completely unnecessary act.

Jesus healed from miles away at times. He healed with words, with mud, with water. This time, Jesus healed with His hand, stretched out. He offered an intimate touch, like you and I have probably done a thousand times for a sick child or loved one in our lives.

Jesus was in the business of healing. And while He healed, in order to show His glory as the Son of God, I also think He healed because he cared. He healed because His heart hurt to see people suffering. And He healed to show us that this was His work. Maybe He heals differently than we would like sometimes, but He does tend to hearts long-broken and scars still in need of tender care.

Jesus. *Jehovah Rapha*. He is ever healing sin in repentance. We walk through life attuned to His Word. He is attentive to our prayers, gathering us around His banquet table. We drink His fresh water, and He is always tending to our hearts and minds.

Dear Lord, only you know where each of us need healing. You, Lord, who came to Simon Peter's Mother-in-Law and reached out. Lord, reach out to us and let us drink deeply of your mercy. Stitch up our hearts where there is need. Tend to our scars. Refresh us, and give us strength where we are tired. You, Jesus, are wonderful, gracious, Savior and ever True. In Your name we pray. Amen.

Exploration
Where have you seen Jesus heal within your church or family?

What would you like to ask God to heal today? (For you or someone else.)

day three
A time to break down

It is so intriguing to me that there does not appear to be a negative-positive, or positive-negative rhythm to the words in Ecclesiastes 3:1-8. Open your Bibles and make a chart that lists the generally negative statements like "a time to kill" on one side and the generally positive statements like "a time to dance" on the other.

Generally negative   Generally positive

Notice, it is not as though the negative in each line is presented before the positive (kill, heal) nor the positive always before the negative (embrace, refrain from embracing)*.

Sit with Ecclesiastes 3:1-8 a moment, quietly. Words have emotion attached to them for most of us. When we read the Bible we can be aware of our own pre-formulated ideas around words, and ask God to open our hearts to hear His Truth through the mire of our life experiences. I think we'll find together, through this study, that God's ways and words aren't always clear cut with positive and negative. There are a whole lot of hues of grey wonderfulness if we can sit back and let God reveal the struggle and the beauty in each little thing.

"Break down" seems at first glance like a negative phrase. Things that come to mind include a nervous breakdown, breaking down of relationships or trust, and breaking down a building that is aged or decrepit.

The Hebrew transliteration of the root word *parats* can be translated: *to tear down, break down, break through, a breach, to break away, an act of violence, an outburst,* or *to press* or *to urge,* or even *to scatter,* or *spread out.*

The use of the same word *parats,* in Genesis 28:10-15, is interesting. Read this passage and see if you can find it, keeping in mind the diversity of meanings in the paragraph above.

What is the promise included in the spreading of this passage?

This is the same root word in verse 14 that is translated *to spread abroad.* Breaking things down sometimes looks like spreading things out. Many of you have moved, many of you have moved more than once. Maybe one of those moves felt like God breaking your heart, or maybe it felt like a new adventure. Maybe it felt like a bit of both. How does the spreading out of family and friends in life feel a little like a breaking down of some kind?

Maybe you feel differently with time and space. Spreading out can be hard, looking out a rearview mirror at family and friends, missing birthday parties and dinners together, trying to make new friends. But how often does spreading out turn into something beautiful? Again, what's the promise?

In the New Testament, we find another scattering. We get the benefit of years and the whole story of history to see the value of this scattering, but I wonder if any of those early disciples were groping for the positive in the negative.

Please read Acts 8:1-4.

Not to overwhelm you with language, but the Greek here for *scattered* is *diasparentes*. This sounds similar enough to me to our Hebrew root to take note. God spreads, God breaks down, God takes bricks of His living stones and builds churches and community and spaces where His Word can be heard and hearts can be filled.

The gift is so often wrapped in paper that doesn't look pretty.

One sunny morning in 2001, Dave and I hiked a mountain in India. We were on a trip for cross-cultural experience with the Seminary. We were matched up with a guide, named Joshua, a professor from the Lutheran Seminary in Nagercoil, India. He was kind and always helpful, seeking our comfort constantly. One morning, we had driven to visit a Hindu temple, eaten lunch off of banana leaves and headed on our way back to our guesthouse. The SUV stopped, Joshua got out and stated as plain as day, "Now we will climb a mountain."

A bit stunned, we climbed out of the vehicle in our flip flops (standard cultural footwear choice), and began hiking. Our fellow travelers eventually dropped like flies over the daunting task of climbing over boulders, and through little crevices, up and up and up. My adventurous spirit warred with my screaming calf muscles, "Give up!" "Where in the world are we going?!" "Is this really worth all this?" "Keep going! You never know!"

An adventurous spirit won. Dave and I blindly followed our seminary guide up the hard and rocky pathway. At 10am on a bright and beautiful Indian morning, we reached the top of this small mountain and our guide announced,

"You see, all around you, these are the roads the Early Christians traveled to escape persecution. These are some of the first areas reached beyond Judea with the Gospel of Christ."

A grueling hike, cramped muscles, heaving breathes. Only beautiful. I could literally feel the great cloud of witnesses that have gone before and stood around me.

What seemingly negative walk have you taken in this life, that God has used to show you His beauty? Where has He shown you Himself, that you may have missed the first time around?

Scattered, broken down, pressed hard, breached. He is working in it all.

May you be blessed today with the knowledge that not only His mercies are new every morning, but His grace is sufficient for each day – good or bad, positive or negative.

Exploration

Go back and ask yourself this question from today's study…
What seemingly negative walk have you taken in this life that
has God shown you His beauty in? Where has He shown
Himself that you may have missed the first time around?

What adventurous thing have you done that at first you
found yourself grumbling over?

-WV mtn climb

- Army wives

day four
A burden that builds

One thing I remember clearly about living in Haiti was the sound of construction – hammers clanking, and concrete being poured, drills and saws working away. So much constructing! It was a wonderful thing. Daily we would walk in the village around our guesthouse and greet a myriad of neighbors and workmen laboring away on a home.

The sounds of construction are more than the sounds of hard work. They are the sounds of a life being built, a family being born, of hope and good health and the stewarding of God's resources. Constructing means action and planning and progressing to something else, to start another season, another chapter of life.

When you look at building in the Old Testament, you will find many passages about building altars, homes, or a city. It is beautiful that all these primary structures still focus on connection and community among people. Through time, God has sustained His people as a people….together, connected, needing and blessing one another, through community.

Perhaps one of the best examples of this is found in the Book of Nehemiah. Nehemiah had a dream, a God-sized dream.

Actually, first, Nehemiah had a burden...a God-sized burden.

Let's read about it! First open the pages of your Bible to read Nehemiah 1:3-4.

Nehemiah's heart broke for those experiencing shame. His heart broke for the people and the city, as well as the weight of sin that brought the present situation. Nehemiah's burden did not go unnoticed. God opened a door through King Artaxerxes. He received supplies and people and headed out on a mission, a mission to build.

Smooth, you say? The reality was not really so smooth. Building up, although prompted and blessed by God, is not without its challenges, as Nehemiah found out. Look further through your pages to read Nehemiah 4:1-6.

That's a giant paragraph full of bullies, but a prayer before God and a mind to do the work was a game changer the bullies never expected. Nehemiah and the people built anyway. They built with eyes fixed on God, who is the very foundation of anything we could even dream of building.

2 Corinthians 4:16-18 reminds us that we fix our eyes on what is unseen, but it is anything but temporary. We'll look at the NIV for its clear word picture. I included this passage below:

> *Therefore we do not lose heart. Though outwardly we are wasting away, yet inwardly we are being renewed day by day. For our light and momentary troubles are achieving for us an eternal glory that far outweighs them all. So we fix our eyes not on what is seen, but on what is unseen, since what is seen is temporary, but what is unseen is eternal.*

Nehemiah and the people built one another up by fixing their eyes not around them, but above them. Nehemiah and his compadres went through a life-changing move, jeers and mocking, a tender heart put to the test, and lived in very real danger to their lives. But in the end, all that mattered was God's faithfulness lived out, in hands ready to put hammer to nails and hearts to prayer.

Nehemiah 7:66 tells us that this project, built up over 40,000 people in the Lord. I'm not sure Nehemiah had that great a number in mind. He was just a guy with a burden...

a God-sized burden.

Because of God's work lived out in Nehemiah and the people, the Feast of Booths was created and celebrated, the Law was read to these 40,000 people in a way that they understood it. I invite you to read through Nehemiah chapter 8. It's worth the time! Write below the people's response to the Word of God read to them that day.

Eventually the temple was rebuilt, God's presence was in the midst of His people, in a tangible way, once again.
What is your God-sized burden? It need not be a city wall to be built. Maybe you desire for your precious child to follow Christ with her whole heart, or you desire for your husband to be filled with renewed joy in his work, or to see people gathering in your home for Bible study, or nursing home residents to be given the small gift of comfort.

What does Ephesians 4:15-16 tell us builds up in the Body of Christ?

Go and build. This is God's work in and through you. This is the church on earth at work, together. Driven by one God-sized gift...Love.

Nehemiah loved God and His people. Nehemiah allowed his heart to be weighed down and stretched out, so that God's ideas and God's love could fill it up. Building a home, building a family, building in our vocations, building up the church – this is our work here in this place and time. May your God-sized burden be blessed, today and always.

Exploration

What burden have you carried or are you currently carrying for His work?

What challenges do you face in carrying out this work?

What do you pray when you come before God about this burden?

day five
Brick by brick…one day at a time

At least five friends of ours have artwork in their homes that depict the city of Chicago in one way or another. I think it's a side effect of attending college in the city – you must have Chicago art. It's an easy city to fall in love with. The sounds of cars and trains compete with the glimmer of glass and steel for your attention, but the rich blue of the lake keeps the outstretched city from becoming too overbearing and stressful. There's something about that water, deep and wide, that holds the city's sanity in check, and your heart in excitement and energy without the racing city running you over with its stress.

One particular piece of artwork shows the city skyline in black and white pieces of newspaper. It's fun and witty, but a part of me always wonders whether we'll need to bring it up to date at some point. A skyline wasn't meant to be stagnant. Sometimes skylines change slowly over time, and sometimes they change in a moment.

We all learned this in the aftermath of September 11th, 2001. The New York skyline was forever changed that day when the twin towers fell. Sin in the world touched our lives and changed a city, many families, a whole nation in a single morning. By God's grace, something new was resurrected in the wake of sorrow, loss, and overwhelming change.

But even without tragedy, cities have a heartbeat and an attitude and with or without help, they will grow and change and take new shape.

We are like cities in this way. We are living and breathing and whether we invite it in or not, life will grow up in us and around us.

We were meant to build, but we were also meant to be built.

1 Peter 2:1-5 speaks to this truth. What is the description of God's people in these verses?

→ Living Stones   → Rejected by men   → Spiritual Infants

While we are building as the church on earth, we ourselves are being built, one day at a time, by a Savior who loves us, and chooses us, and grows good things in us – Love and Forgiveness, Compassion and Grace.

You, my friend, are a holy house, a residence of the Almighty God, but He is not done building you. You are a temple of the Holy Spirit. He lives in you, breathes in you, and does His work in and through you. Brick by brick, in this life, He is perfecting you in ways that only He knows about. He reveals Himself to you in His Word and adds another stone. He adds some mortar called relationship and sticks us to our neighbor and together we grow. Name some people, places, blessings, or challenges that God has used to build you.

Sometimes the growth process is easy. We read, try, or discover something new and it's all joy and excitement. Sometimes the growth process is hard. Broken dreams, a shattered relationship, a painful conversation containing reality and Truth. After all, sometimes things need to be broken down for something new to be built up. Just imagine what we look like to God, who holds the blueprint! I stand in the promise that the end result is something He calls not just good, but very good. And in all of it, we are living stones, like that living city, teeming with life, but filled with the deep blue waters of peace that passes all understanding.

Lord, work in us. Build us, mold us, shape us; not just as individuals, but as Your people, your priesthood. We offer our lives to Your care and Your work. Thank you for Jesus, the perfect Cornerstone, who holds us all up and together. In His name we pray. Amen!

The Read Aloud Family

Exploration

How is God building you in this present season? What is He constructing and working on in your life and in your heart?

What kinds of things need to go, need to be broken down in order for the new to be built up?

Who is God mortaring you to? What relationships do you hear Him calling you to spend a bit more time on?

mourning,
dancing, and
everything
in between

week four

Mourning, Dancing, and Everything in Between
Ecclesiastes 3:4

Noisy, messy crying
Chuckles, giggling, and other fun things
Permission to mourn
Keeping the party alive
Kids songs, chanting, and Biblical randomness

heart verse

When Jesus saw her weeping, and the Jews who had come with her also weeping, he was deeply moved in his spirit and greatly troubled.
                    John 11:33

mourning, dancing, and everything in between

day one
Noisy, messy crying (A time to weep)

Several years ago, while my sister was visiting from Iowa, some friends stopped by and we decided to watch a movie. It was the kind of night when all the stars align and small people go to bed on time and you think, "You know what I could really go for? A blanket, some popcorn, and a good movie." We sat down to watch the latest new release, *7 Pounds*, with Will Smith. It was a well-filmed movie. Good characters, creative plot, interesting dialogue.

And absolutely depressing.

We all watched the movie, completely riveted. When the closing credits began to roll, I woke up from my movie stupor to the sound of sobbing. In about four seconds, I realized the sound was coming from me. Wait, no, it's coming from Dave...and our friend...and our other friend...and my sister. Our living room was filled with dazed and confounded individuals crying their eyes out, noisily. Messy. There wasn't a dry eye in the house. There was also snot running out of noses and slobber rubbed onto shirt sleeves, and sobs bursting out from weird facial convulsions. It was bad. It was ugly-cry bad.

Days later, I was still analyzing our universally embarrassing, no-holds-barred reaction to this movie. The film was great, but the reality was that the topic was disturbing and frustrating and left you longing to help, but nothing could be done. These people were actors on a screen, playing a part, but all of us had the startling revelation that in this case, fiction closely mirrored reality. The plot may be fiction, but the mindset encapsulated in the movie is far from it. People misunderstand law and justice and grace so much, that they can miss eternity for want of finding it. This movie was the truth of our culture spoken in technicolor –

There are many who don't know Jesus, who need Jesus. They long for healing and rescue from heartbreak. Unfortunately, not a single person on the road of searching the main character walked, not one, told him what he longed to hear...*the message of grace, redemption.*

All of us, sitting in that room, noisy crying, were left wondering if we had so utterly failed someone in our own lives. Our cries were prayers for God to fill in the gaps where we are weak. To send His Word into the lives of those around us, when we had been silent.

Let's look at our passage for the week again. Write Ecclesiastes 3:4 below.

The Hebrew root word found in Ecclesiastes 3:4 for *a time to weep*, *bakah*, is phonetically pronounced *bawkaw*. Sound familiar? The immediate phrase that came to my mind when I heard it was *to bawl*.

That's the way my dad always referred to the noisy, messy crying when, as little kids, one of us was just completely inconsolable, or "bawling our eyes out." This kind of crying, or weeping as Ecclesiastes calls it, is a kind of emotional release.

Sometimes we need to cry. We need to move our internal emotions to the external, because they are just so much to bear. Tears and, even more so, weeping give us the ability to express the inexpressible, to unload the ugly, messy anxiety and emotion stuck inside of us. Weeping is not simply a negative experience of difficult emotion. It is a cry that is mostly between us and God. We cry out in a sacred prayer, hidden in the depths of our sobs,

"It's too much, Lord. It's too much."

Joseph experienced this kind of emotional overload in Genesis 42:1-24. Please read this account and list all of the people involved.

When his brothers arrive in the midst of the famine, Joseph creates a plan for discernment and handles the situation, from the reader's perspective in a well thought out manner. Then it happens. He overhears his brothers make a confession. One little sentence, that they think he cannot understand...

Reread Genesis 42:24.

Joseph sat in a *bawkaw* prayer, "It's too much, Lord. It's too much."

I'm guessing at this point in the family drama, Joseph is overrun with emotions. Joy and dread and fear and childhood trauma; the emotions of a soul hungry for vengeance but whispering grace and restoration.

Mary and Martha knew "it's just too much" well. In John 11:32-35, we read a tiny piece of the Lazarus story. Underline any word that expresses emotion in this passage below.

> Now when Mary came to where Jesus was and saw him, she fell at his feet, saying to him, "Lord, if you had been here, my brother would not have died."
>
> When Jesus saw her weeping, and the Jews who had come with her also weeping, he was deeply moved in his spirit and greatly troubled. And he said, "Where have you laid him?"
>
> They said to him, "Lord, come and see."
>
> Jesus wept.
>
> So the Jews said, "See how he loved him!"
>
> But some of them said, "Could not he who opened the eyes of the blind man also have kept this man from dying?"

Who wept? Mary wept. Martha wept. Jesus wept. He hears the cries of a heart tender with grief and is moved to not just tears, but to weep as well. This means God himself has wept as we have wept. He has lost friends. He has shared grief. He has had His soul overwhelmed with sorrow, as a man. Will He not then hear us when it's just too much? Yes, He will!

When we feel the need to cry those messy tears, let us do so unashamed. We can present them to Him as an offering of prayer:

"Lord, it's a lot. I lay this burden on You. The one who is fully capable of bearing the load. In my weakness, Your strength. You invite me, saying, 'Hand it here, child. The burden is mine to carry.'"

Messy tears, snot pouring out, unattractive sobs escaping...these are all a part of a life fully lived, abundantly lived in the One who collects my tears and holds me while I weep.

Exploration

Read Revelation 5:1-5. What promise does God hold in these verses for weeping and crying?

When was a time you remember having a messy, noisy cry? Was it warranted?

mourning, dancing, and everything in between

day two
Chuckles, giggling, and other fun things

You would think laughing would be a positive day in this Bible study. I like a good laugh. I don't fancy myself a comedian, but I tend towards making light of things to ease the darkness of life. I like to see people smile and getting them to laugh is a special bonus that I admit I enjoy.

The root word for laugh in Ecclesiastes 3:4 is funny sounding to me in itself...*sawkawk*.

I imagine an unattractive bird with a long turkey skin neck and beady eyes strutting around yelling, "*Sawkawk! Sawkawk!*" Too funny.

The Hebrew root *sachaq* – pronounced *sawkawk* – can mean *to make sport*, *to jest*, *to laugh*, or *to amuse*...it appears that there is a time for humor, and there most certainly is! However, I was shocked to find that most uses in the Bible of this root are, what I would consider, on the negative side of things.

There is a fair amount of derision in the Old Testament. People laughing at others, expressions of the Psalmist laughing at us, individual and communal angst expressed when someone is made fun of for another's pleasure and gain. There is the time when both Abraham and Sarah laugh at God (not a great move), and even in Proverbs 31 she – wisdom, or the proverbial woman – laughs at time, like, "Hey time, take that! You think you can foil me, watch my tornado-self clean this house and play with these kids and love on this husband." You get the idea.

In the New Testament, we often see the Pharisees laughing at Jesus. This is not good laughter either. Bad move, Pharisees. But Jesus, as He so often does, turns the things of this world on their ear.

Please read Luke 6:20-26.

Don't miss the beauty in verse 20 – *"And he lifted up his eyes on his disciples..."*

He had a particular audience for this passage. We also are His disciples. He ever invites us into relationship with Him and he's honest with us.

> *Blessed are you who weep...*

There will be weeping, but they will laugh.

> *Woe to those who laugh...*

They will weep. Oh, will they weep.

It's a promise with some wisdom tucked in. Not to be too law-oriented, but it begs the question – what is funny to us? Is it appropriate? Is it at the expense of someone else?

When we laugh in eternity it will be sheer joy. Eternity is the joyous reward promised. Joy will burst forth in all places and spaces. God gives us glimpses and moments of that with those we love now. We laugh at our child making silly faces to amuse us, we laugh at an ironic coincidence on a TV show, we laugh at a friend's perfect timing when they share, "I have totally been there!"

One thing I learned from reading the Scriptures today is that I have a new prayer.

I thank you, Lord, for laughter, and for people to share moments and time and pleasures with. Lord, keep my heart from finding humor in someone else's struggle. Mold me and make me tender to Your precious people. May I always laugh, but may it never be at someone else's expense. May even my laughter point to You. In Your Name we pray, Amen.

Exploration

What makes you laugh? (This is a no judgement zone! Be honest. A person, a show, a limerick, whatever.)

Share a joke or something funny with your group, or recall one for yourself.

Do you have any painful memories of someone laughing at you or a time you treated someone poorly that you wish you could undo? (Take a deep breath and breathe in God's forgiveness in His Word!)

day three
Permission to mourn

Please note: today's lesson discusses the topic of rape and sexual trauma. If you have experienced any kind of sexual trauma, please know that it is ok if you prefer not to read today's devotion. There are great resources and crisis hotlines for help also available at rainn.org.

Remember in Day One of this week's study, when we talked about weeping? You may be wondering why the need to discuss mourning two days later? On Day One, we highlighted the overload of emotions associated with weeping. Tears can come for any number of reasons. Mourning, on the other hand, is connected to grief and loss. The Hebrew root in Ecclesiastes 3 for mourn is *saphad* and is intimately connected with loss. You can fix in your mind a picture of traditional Biblical lamenting – *weeping, beating of the breast, tearing of hair, sackcloth and ashes.*

2 Samuel 13 has one of the most painful stories we can find in Scripture. There is more lamenting in one chapter than I can begin to wrap my head around. This Bible story is PG-13 for sure, so be warned. I'm going to ask you to dig your Bibles out and read 2 Samuel 13 in its entirety. Again,

it's distressing, but something to remember is that God sees. He sees someone's struggle. He sees the painful things and has chosen to include these things in His Word, and by that we can know that He sees even the hardest things we experience. His care, His redemption is always the answer for our deepest pain.

This is a story of rape. This is also the experience of human shame, despair, rage, and a family broken. You can see the reason for so much lamenting. It is an entirely appropriate response to what is taken, what is lost, and what is broken.

In verse 18, Tamar weeps and cries aloud. She puts ashes on her head. In verse 31, King David is mourning the mistaken information that all His sons are dead. In verse 36, all David's servants join him in mourning the loss of Absalom. This is family heartache, household trauma. When things like this happen, they are not simple. They are not an individual loss, rather they very much affect the entire family, the entire community.

Have you lost something you have mourned in such a way? Maybe there is something you are currently mourning. We may not put on sackcloth and ashes, but lamenting is not less because it is done quietly. The thing that makes mourning what it is and sets it apart from crying, is acknowledging there is a loss. And this action is oh-so important.

The Jewish act of lamenting was often within the context of a *time* set aside for mourning. There are seasons in life when we need just that...time. We need time to heal. Time to think. Time to sort. Time to rest. Within the Christian context of the Body of Christ, this also means that we are invited to a time of comfort from those around us.

Christ's comfort comes out of each of us into one another. 2 Corinthians 7:5-7 tells us that comfort is part of the life of the Body. Read these verses and circle the forms of the word comfort that you find.

> *For even when we came into Macedonia, our bodies had no rest, but we were afflicted at every turn—fighting without and fear within. But God, who comforts the downcast, comforted us by the coming of Titus, and not only by his coming but also by the comfort with which he was comforted by you, as he told us of your longing, your mourning, your zeal for me, so that I rejoiced still more.*

Who does God use in this passage to offer comfort to the writer and his fellow missionaries?

Why did they need comfort?

His comfort, found in one another. How precious is that! Who around you is hurting? Who around you need rest? Maybe the hurt in this season is your own; what kind of comfort do you need? Our loss may be the death of someone we love, the loss of a childhood due to trauma, or even the loss of what we thought our lives would look like at this stage. There is no loss too small for His comfort, and His comfort is never small. Christ's comfort fills up and overflows, sister. So much more than a warm baggy sweater and a mug of green tea on a rainy day, Christ gives us one another and Himself through one another.

Rape is certainly worth lamenting. **It is also worth comforting.**

We NEED one another in times like Tamar experienced. We need to share our secret shame, even when the shame is a product of someone else's sin. When we rush head on into the fear within and struggle like Absalom; we NEED brothers and sisters that will come after us and restore, restore, restore. We have a Father who does that. Mourn what is deserving of mourning, and honor the one mourning by sitting beside them in the darkness.

And please rest in this:

whatever your lament is, He redeems even that.

No doubt about it. He says it over and over in His Word. Nothing is outside of His Grace, outside of His restoration. He redeems each and every thing in our lives.

Exploration
Where do you see the need for comfort in our world today?

Who around you is hurting?

Name simple ways to give comfort when someone is hurting.

What difficult situation have you seen Christ redeem?

mourning,
dancing, and
everything
in between

day four
Keeping the party alive

A well-known fact in our congregation is that my husband and I love to dance. I remember one of the first weddings my husband officiated. It was hot, middle-of-July-no-air-conditioning-in-the-church hot. We all would have been happy with bologna sandwiches at the reception, because of the cool, sweet blowing air coming from magical vents in the ceiling. I think everyone attributed our moves on the dance floor to air-conditioned rejoicing, and we shut the dance floor down.

At the next wedding reception, people started to comment.
"Enjoying yourselves?!"
"Look at you go! So much fun!"
And my personal favorite...
"Wow! You guys can really cut a rug!"

Dave and I are naturally less inhibited in one another's company. Something about having someone that loves you so wholeheartedly brings out the party simmering on the inside. Give us a dance floor and we crank it to "a whole nother level."

Now, do not be mistaken. We have no real moves. I mean we barely have pretend moves. We have a tiny bit of rhythm. And in college we took a 6 session class on ballroom dancing, but we are in no way even worthy of watching "So You Think You Can Dance."

What we do have is a lot of joy. And it's not just average run of the mill joy, it's Jesus in the midst of His people joy. I think one of the reasons wedding receptions are so exciting for us, is that we are elated to be allowed into these people's lives. It is sheer blessing to not only witness new love, but to be a part of building it up for the months before the wedding, and to look forward to the years to come of new homes and tiny babies and joy and heartache. Just to be a part of it and experience life together is amazing. What a life we have! Psalm 149 is chock full of this kind of Joy. Let's read it! Please share some of the words or phrases from the psalm that speak joy to you.

He is worthy, so worthy.

Matthew Henry tells us in his commentary that his "guess" is that this psalm of praise was "penned upon occasion of *some* victory." I love that. *Some victory*. Life is full of random little victories, pieced together, and we are blest as believers to be the ones who can look victory in the face and say "That's Jesus. Right there. That's Jesus."

Weddings, babies, graduations, new ideas, a meal well served, time spent in refreshing conversation that builds up, words tamped down and spoken carefully instead of with unconstrained rage, getting to church on time with 4 small people in tow. *Some victory*.

There are so many things in life worth dancing and praising. David danced before the Lord (2 Samuel 6). Miriam and the women danced before Him after crossing through the Red Sea (Exodus 15). Israel's mourning is promised to be turned to dancing (Jeremiah 31).

All of these dances, if you notice, are completely and utterly communal. I love to dance it up in my house while I'm dusting as much as the next girl, but there is nothing like sharing the joy, sharing the victories of life, with the Body. Share it. Celebrate it, together.

Exploration
What things in life just make you want to dance?

What victories, big or small, are you able to sit back and praise Jesus for?

Who has shared in these victories with you?

day five

Kids songs, chanting, and Biblical randomness

My children have this thing with clapping and chanting. I can take each one separately...clapping at an event or in excitement; chanting Matins, or even "We want cookies!" or some nonsense. I cannot take the two combined. You know the sound. Little girls gathering together on the playground doing some hand jive with repetitive words. Kids love that stuff, but I don't. At some point I holler, "Enough already!"

Maybe my weirdness about children's playground chants is why the verses we're studying today stuck out to me, when I was searching the Scriptures about dancing. These verses are in red letters, which makes most of us sit up a little straighter. I'll warn you, it took me two good days and a few commentaries to even begin to formulate what in the world Jesus is saying with a children's chant.

Let's read Matthew 11:7-19 (the parallel is found in Luke 7 if you'd like to compare the two). After you've read, write the chant Jesus refers to in Matthew 11:17, in the space below.

Notice that Matthew 11:17 addresses both dancing and mourning, the same as we find in our Ecclesiastes passage. That doesn't mean that the two passages are specifically connected, but it does mean that it is useful to look at them side by side.

Jesus speaks in Matthew about John, but he's really addressing the crowd concerning their faith. He asks them what they came for. What was their motivation in coming to hear John preach and teach? He then outlines the basis for John's preaching and teaching. He points to the Old Testament as a voice that bears the Truth concerning who John is and more importantly, who John is in relation to Jesus.

Verse 16 gets blunt. "But..."

Uh-oh. You know that kind of *but*. I use that kind of but as a mom. "I gave you everything you needed to succeed. I made you a chore chart. I laid out all your clothes. I bought prepackaged snacks. BUT... we still cannot make it to school on time?!"

The *but* of Matthew 11:16 is a what-in-the-world-happened *but*. Jesus even uses that sort of phrasing.

"To what shall I compare this generation..."

It's as if Jesus is saying, "Where do I even start? How can I help you understand yourselves?" So, Jesus uses a familiar children's song of the day in verse 17, to help them understand. He uses this song as a parable of sorts.

Jesus compares the people of His time to a generation of children sitting around chanting and playing on the playground. Some of them (Jesus, John, the disciples) are doing their thing, playing instruments, singing. The crowd, however, is full of the people who look at them, stare at them, but do nothing. They refuse to join in. They just sit and watch. They look at them as though their song makes no sense, their instruments are out of place. They choose nothing over the Gospel. They choose nothing over a life changed by grace.

You see, children love chants and songs, evidently this was as true in 20AD-ish as it is in the twenty-first century. When my children sing and laugh and clap together, other children inevitably run over and desire fervently to learn the ditty. This is normal behavior.

John preached, Jesus taught. They were authentic and genuine and true to the Word of the prophets and the teachers of the Law. They were the real deal, but all the people wanted to do was watch in confusion and contempt. This is *not* normal behavior when you hear the life changing message of Christ Jesus. This is choosing nothing. This is seeing Jesus reaching out and walking away, rather than letting Him set His free gift of grace in your lap.

Jesus offers us so much. He offered us His very self on the cross. He walked out of a tomb and ascended to His Father in the heavens...so that we could LIVE.

Jesus, in this passage, invites us to LIVE. Whether that is in songs of praise and dancing, or returning week after week hungry for His Word, or sharing mercy with those around us. *He placed His Spirit in us so that we can, in fact, respond.*

When we engage in worship, when we reach out to our brother; when we eat at His table, we are living and breathing Who He is to the next generation and to our own generation. We need not be the generation of Jesus' day, watchers on the sidelines. We are Spirit-filled believers in a Holy and Living God. Praise the Lord!

Let us go and respond. What does that look like for you today? I don't know. It looks different for you than it looks for me and that's a beautiful thing.

But let us Live with a capital L. Let us sing when Jesus plays His music of Grace, respond with words of repentance and sorrow when we see our own sin, and dance when He extends His ever-present mercy.

I'm singing and dancing with you today, sisters, in Jesus' precious Name.

Exploration
What chants do you remember from childhood?

What was your favorite Jesus song to sing as a child?

What are some ways we are blessed to be able to respond to Jesus' love and care for us?

the gift of
relationship

week five

The Gift of Relationship
Ecclesiastes 3:5

Casting away stones
We gather together
Christians don't shake hands, Christians gotta hug!
Boundaries and margins and the in-between
Another kind of refraining

heart verse
I will make my dwelling among them
and walk among them,
and I will be their God,
and they shall be my people.
2 Corinthians 6:16b

day one

Casting away stones

Just over halfway through our study, we arrive at the title passage.

Casting away stones...

Why this title? Why out of all the things we have been studying in Ecclesiastes, did this particular metaphor stick out when I was digging deeper?

Well, first, it is interesting that the phrase *cast away* is used twice in Ecclesiastes 3. Open your Bibles and find both by reading Ecclesiastes 3:5-6.

Things that make you go hmmmmm...

Second, the phrase simply spoke to my heart. It was what drew my eye back to the passage time and again, asking questions and searching. I have had a sense for a while that God was teaching me about the seasonal aspects of life. My family has had our adventures with seasons! I bet many of you have also. Have you ever had a time in the Word when God spoke by highlighting a passage or phrase?

Casting away brings to mind mental images of fishermen casting nets or the fly fishermen in the movie *A River Runs Through It* sending their line out and casting it back in. There is a rhythm to it, standing in the water, casting back and forth, back and forth, until a catch is found.

In Ecclesiastes 3:5-6, God tells us that there is a time for *casting away stones* and a time to *gather stones together*. This second phrase is actually essential in understanding the first phrase. If we are gathering stones together, then the casting away of stones is a bit different. Bear with me here. There is no way of actually knowing, nor does it completely matter if we understand the exact phrasing. This is not an issue of salvation, but worthy of contemplation.

At first, when I read the words *casting away*, I thought the passage was speaking of throwing stones away, like you would throw away a banana peel, or take a shirt you are done wearing to the Goodwill. The Hebrew for *casting away* can mean exactly that, and does mean that, as you will see in next week's passage. However, here we have the casting away immediately compared to bringing stones together. In my mind, the word *together* transforms verse 5 from being about stuff and things, to being about the relationship between the items.

Gathering stones together…

Do you hear the relationship in that phrase of the stones one to another?

There is a time to gather and there is a time to cast what needs to be cast. This is different than a throwing away of a relationship or a person. I'm not sure God ever calls us, even while using extremely tight boundaries (we'll address boundaries in day 4) to throw people away. Our verses in Ecclesiastes speak more to the idea that there is a time to be together, to gather together, and there is a time to spread out, to be apart.

If you have ever moved in your life, you understand the idea of spreading out. If you have moved more than once, you understand it all the more. We went to the Seminary for three years, vicarage in Nebraska for one year, we were Ohioans for more than twelve years, spent a brief fall in Haiti, grew up in Michigan and Missouri, and now we are Nebraskans again. That means that my heart is divided between many states. We have friends in Texas, Colorado, Arizona, Minnesota, New York, Africa, Haiti, etc., etc. I could keep going.

Spreading out is not easy. There are people who are part of our very heart that we will never live next door to. It's just our reality. God tells us here in Ecclesiastes that there is a time for this. There are times and places and people in our lives that He is asking us to cast away from. Not to throw those relationships overboard, but to cast out from one another on the strange adventure of life, sharing His message in each of our places. Like stones in a field, you find one believer here, one over there, and another along the creek.

If I were in charge I would have all the people I love in one field, all huddled together in a big pile of love, but who would reach Texas then? And who would minister in Jacmel? Who would bring Him to the people of Minnesota?

This also holds true in the context of your local congregation. There are times when we can gather and come together and love on each other – worship, Bible study, youth night, potlucks, VBS week, small groups, community coffee. But there are also times when we are meant to be cast out into our community, out from our homes and our comfortable spaces, to meet someone new, to shine a little light in a different place.

The disciples knew a little more about stones than we do. They lived with the threat of actual stoning shadowing their life every day, and each time we read about them, they are being spread out. Let's read about one instance in Acts 13:48-52.

Can you find the rhythm? Find for me the blessings of Gospel fruit, given by God, along with the rejoicing in the beginning of the passage, followed by the persecution. Now find the persecution of faith, followed again by the blessings and joy. If you have your Bible open, underline the persecution you find in one color and the rejoicing in another color. This rhythm is so Ecclesiastes-like, pointing to the seasons of life.

God works in the gathering, but he also works in the spreading, or the "casting away." We are His living stones, not His sitting dormant stones. May we ever let Him cast us near and far, in the comfortable places and the uncomfortable places.

Until we gather tomorrow, dear sisters, thank you for studying with me from your place in His kingdom field.

Exploration
Just for fun, if you could live anywhere, where would you choose to live?

To what places and to what people have you been cast during your lifetime?

Have you ever had the experience of a Scripture passage that keeps drawing your attention? If so, what passage and how did it speak to you?

the gift of
relationship

day two
We gather together

We gather together to ask the Lord's blessing;
He chastens and hastens His will to make known;
the wicked oppressing now cease from distressing.
Sing praises to His name; He forgets not his own.

(We Gather Together – public domain)

Do you know this song? Can you hear the hymn in your head? I was reading Scripture and commentary to get ready for this post and I just could not get this particular hymn out of my brain. The hymn is traditionally a thanksgiving hymn, but was originally used for patriotic purposes by the Dutch. The last time I heard it, it was played for a baptism.

I watched the darling baby being baptized and I sat back and listened. I didn't sing. I just listened. In fact, I entered that weird vortex when everything seems to go still around you and it's just you and God. Except it wasn't. It was me and God and the voices of a hundred of God's precious people singing praise to His name.

Beside us to guide us, our God with us joining,
ordaining, maintaining His kingdom divine;
so from the beginning the fight we were winning;
Thou, Lord, wast at our side; all glory be Thine!

(We Gather Together – public domain)

Beside us, joining, maintaining, at our side. Gathering
together Scripturally is almost always about relationship.
This made it a perfect hymn for baptism – baptism, after all,
is all about relationship!

Let's look at Ecclesiastes 3:5 to refresh our memory
regarding the wording...
> a time to cast away stones, and a time to gather
> stones together;
> a time to embrace, and a time to refrain from
> embracing;

The counter to casting away stones from yesterday's study
is to gather stones together.

Let's see what we can learn about gathering from Scripture.
Today is a full study day! There are a lot of Scriptures to dig
through. Feel free to do it in more than one sitting if that suits
your schedule and your brain better. Let the Word sit or
plunge ahead! For now, let's open our Bibles and check out
the following passages. Challenge yourself to dig in! Next to
the passage reference, write who is involved and what kind
of gathering of stones is happening in each one.

Genesis 25:8

Genesis 31:43-55

1 Kings 18:19-20

Ezra 3:1

Isaiah 11:12

Mark 2:2

John 11:51-53

Acts 13:44-45

2 Thessalonians 2:1

The people and things in these Scriptures were not simply collected and placed haphazardly. These people were gathered together for a purpose, whether to unite as His people, or by Him as the diaspora (scattered people), or even in order to plot against Him. Even those enemy hands are gathered together by God's hand and providence.

One of my favorite stories of gathering is in Esther 4. Please read this whole chapter for context. Pay special attention to Esther 4:10-17.

Write out Mordecai's wisdom for Esther in verse 13-14 below:

The account of Esther is all at once familiar and confusing for many of us. It has a lot of names and "he said, she said". This can serve to remind us that God values all people. He sees us as individuals, but He also sees us as a community of His people.

When we stand together as Christians, we stand as the Body of Christ. We are not living our lives for only ourselves, but for one another. And each of you are being lived for, by your Christian brothers and sisters. The great cloud of witnesses isn't just a fun picture of the saints gone before us and the saints around us. It is a living and active, breathing ministry, to the whole Church...to you, beloved.

Look around you. Who are you here for in this time and place? Who is God gathering you to and with?

The historical account of Esther gives us a glimpse of a moment when God's people were all gathered together for the needs of the body. Reread Esther 4:16. Circle the word *gather* and underline the word following it below.

> Then Esther told them to reply to Mordecai, "Go, gather all the Jews to be found in Susa, and hold a fast on my behalf, and do not eat or drink for three days, night or day. I and my young women will also fast as you do. Then I will go to the king, though it is against the law, and if I perish, I perish."

One for all and all for one. Sometimes persecution brings scattering, and sometimes it brings complete and utter unity, all for Him.

What has God asked of you in your time and place? How do the desires He has laid on your heart, or the tasks He has given you, gather you with His people?

In the end, we, like Abraham, will be gathered together with the saints in Him, perfect and whole and complete. Until then, let us spur one another on – casting living stones and gathering them together, all in His time.

Exploration

What has God asked of you in your time and place?

What strength do you find in *gathering* as a work done with the Body of Christ rather than something God calls you to do on your own? What tools does He give His people for gathering through the Holy Spirit?

the gift of
relationship

day three
Christians don't shake hands, Christians gotta hug!

Many people would call me a hugger. Gracious people sweetly have described one of my finer points as being warm and enthusiastic. I have heard people call me things like bubbly and energetic...most of the time at least. Don't worry, I stay humble. I am also a person way too quick to speak, impatient, and I'm almost always late.

I do like a loving touch, a hand on the shoulder, a touch to the arm, but in reality I am just plain awkward with a hug. I can never figure out when to offer them!

- ♥ I spontaneously must hug you if you are sad.
- ♥ If I see you after a long time, that seems hug-worthy.
- ♥ If you share something personal and deep and I can see the vulnerability written all over the conversation, you'll get a hug.
- ♥ Small children – definitely huggable.
- ♥ Professional relationships that involve ministry – maybe a hug???
- ♥ Narthex chatting on any given Sunday – to hug or not to hug?
- ♥ Random acquaintance/friend in the grocery store, who says "Hi!" with gusto – hug? Yes? No?

You can see my dilemma. Am I the only one? Please say no. Have you ever felt awkward in a hug? If you have an example to share, please do!

Our Ecclesiastes passage today tells us that there is a time to embrace and a time to refrain from embracing. We'll get to the refraining tomorrow, but today, let's own the embracing.

Read Ecclesiastes 3:5 to refresh your memory.

What a beautiful word – embrace. Maybe circle it in your Bible or write it oversized below.

Embrace is a word that exudes much more meaning than the English word "hug". The rich Hebrew root word certainly means to hug, but it can also mean to clasp or to fold. Visualize that for a second, being folded into your favorite person. Who are you thinking of? Tell us about them.

My Aunt Sheila was a tall and regal woman. She was beautiful. She had prematurely grey hair my whole life. For many years her hair was long, and as a child, I imagined her spending hours combing through it. When she hugged me, I felt like I became part of her. She wrapped one arm around me and drew me in. Her hair settled on my shoulders and face like little caresses. It felt safe and warm. I wanted to live in that embrace, away from the scary world.

There are times for embracing, even when we're not hugging people. Can you sit back and think of a few of those times? Who has held you and kept you safe from the world for even a moment? Who has offered an affectionate embrace at just the right time?

There is a woman in the Old Testament longing for another kind of embrace. Her story is both sweet and heartbreaking. It's a long passage, but I promise you, it is oh so worth it! Please read 2 Kings 4:8-37. Make a few notes about who is in the story and what happened to them here.

Here is this woman. She prepares a place in her home, she opens her heart to this stranger, this man she knows is of God, from God. She has no expectations. She simply serves with her whole heart. Elijah asks her, "What can I give you for all you have given me?" (My paraphrase.) Elijah's servant has to share her need for her. Praise God for the people in our lives who speak up for us when we cannot, for those who notice our needs!

Elijah's prophecy is so beautiful to me. It is not that she will conceive and bear a son, or that she will simply give birth to a son. Fill in the blank below.

"At this season, about this time next year, you

shall_____ a son." And she said, "No,

my lord, O man of God; do not lie to your

servant." (v.16)

This prophesy cuts to the heart, so much so that the woman sits in the place of trust-distrust that we so often sit with God. I know you are True, God. I know that you are grace, God. But this...this thing, do not lie to me.

We know with all our heart that He is not even capable of a lie, but part of the walk of growing in faith is trust-distrust.

When your arms are empty, when you are too afraid to pray it or dream it or hope it...whether that looks like miscarriage, or infertility, or loss and grief, a diagnosis, divorce, a broken relationship…any of it…God promises He enfolds us. He embraces us.

He knows when we do not.

And then when dreams come true and the world still shatters around us. Hold fast.

This Shunammite woman, she has been there. Rewrite the Shunammite woman's trust-distrust question of faith from 2 Kings 4:28 below.

In this story there is another kind of embracing. The healing of this precious child is so personal, it steals my breath. Elijah lays on the child,
mouth to mouth
eye to eye
hand to hand.

When we are in that place of trust-distrust, when we are in need, when we feel lost, alone, and maybe even a little bitter or overwhelmed: God sends His people to physically show us Himself. The Body of Christ folds itself around us and pray and feed and remind us of who He is, holding it up before us.

I can't think of anything more like an embrace than that.

And maybe it isn't a desperate sort of time for you. Maybe the warmth of an embrace in this season is fun and spontaneous and not because of burden, but a way to communicate affection and connection. Maybe you are the aunt who folds a frightened child in your arms, or the friend who invites someone to clasp your hand. Whatever the style or season, know that it any genuine love we receive or give is His work. The Lord is at work in His people.

Jesus, you are in the hugs. You are in the warmth and caring. You are in the words of affirmation and edification we receive in one another. May we ever be a source of Your genuineness, Your caring, and Your kind embrace. In Your Holy Name we pray, Amen.

Exploration

Who has offered you memorable hugs in this life?

Have you ever experienced a season of emptiness or deep longing for something? How did you see God work in that time? Who did God send to tend to you?

Do you have any current hopes or dreams? Do you feel like God is asking you to embrace them or do you feel it is a time to step back and refrain?

day four
Boundaries and margins
and the in-between

The term boundaries has become something of a buzzword in our current culture. My generation (can you guess how old I am?!) has been inundated since college with the lingo of boundaries. The trouble with boundaries is that they are pretty easy to talk about, slightly harder to define, and much more difficult to put into practice. My friend, Ali, reminded me of the newer terminology "margins" which is a little different from hard and fast boundaries, so let's do a little word discovery. Look up and define each of the following words from a dictionary – hard back, online, or whatever way you look things up.

Boundary is defined as:

Margin is defined as:

Can you see the difference? Boundaries are something that you define very clearly. There is definitely a time for this. However, margins are a little less defined, but they do create space between two people in order for healthy relationships to exist. They are a little more fluid though. In most cases, the definition of margin includes a *degree* of difference. When we exist in relationship with others we have to constantly be evaluating what is healthy, what is godly, and what is simply not. Sometimes this is clear-cut, and sometimes this is not so clear-cut.

The Hebrew word, *lirhoq,* that translates as *refrain from embracing* can help us understand this matter better. It can be translated *to shun, to keep distance between, or to wholly abstain.* In other words, it's not always cut-and-dry.

Sometimes we wholly abstain – we say no to a relationship, we walk away and don't look back, we wipe the dust off our feet. Other times we need to put distance between us and a friend, a family member or an acquaintance. We need to refrain for a time until the relationship or the parties involved, including ourselves, are in a different place. Sometimes our refraining is very short lived – a night, a day, even a moment or a conversation. Sometimes my husband and I need to walk away from one another for a period of time to cool off and come together again on a given subject. Sometimes someone we care about has a season of wild living, like the prodigal son, and we have no choice but to wave as they walk down the road and pray for God to bring them back to us whole again.

Beyond *lirhoq,* how does the Bible speak of boundaries and margins? First, tell me what you've learned on the subject of boundaries and margins.

What Biblical teaching would you apply to this topic?

We could talk about this subject all day, but to keep it reasonable, let's look at 3 margins that surely fit in our space here.

There is a place for *do not* in our relationships.
Read through 2 Corinthians 6:14-16. What "do not" instruction do you find in this passage?

What exactly does this passage mean?

I think you could find as many suggestions about this as there are commentaries, but I will tell you what I tell my youth group: Jesus ate with tax collectors. Jesus ate with sinners. Jesus would eat with you and me in our darkest moments. But we are not Jesus. We have to understand what relationships we are capable of, that still allow us to flourish and grow in our faith. We need to welcome people into our lives. It's also helpful for us to know and understand our relationship with God in the context of our relationships with those people.

Marriage to an unbeliever, knowingly, willingly, with eyes wide open? Let's take that off the table right now. (Already married to an unbeliever? That is a different story, for a different conversation. Know that God has a plan and He also provides grace to work in it.) Absolute best friends, someone you go to for your most intimate problems, seeking discernment and advice? Also off the table.

You cannot share your entire heart and soul with someone who does not, in fact, share your Heart and Soul.

Jesus is my everything. He is the air I breath and the Lord of my heart, my mind, and all my being. I can love you. I can eat with you. I can share with you. I can honor you as a friend, but there will always be those margins of faith and purpose between us, because you do not know what I know or believe in the God I follow. We do not seek the same things. We do not run to the same well in our desert places. That does not, **does not** mean, I do not value you and hold you in *absolute* high esteem. That does mean there is a barrier to deeper intimacy.

Jesus was genuine about his relationships.
Banking off the first margin, Jesus responded to people in truth. He responded to the Pharisees in truth. He responded to Pontius Pilate in truth. He responded to sinners, like you and me, in truth. He never pretended to admire and seek relationship with someone who wasn't in it for an honest relationship. Neither was he hurtful, rude, or inconsiderate. Jesus truly embodied "speaking the truth in love." Read one example of Jesus's honesty in relationship from John 8:4-11. How is Jesus honest? How is He caring? What boundaries or margins does he maintain?

Jesus embodies an open heart, but never forgets truth.
Jesus sometimes spent time with one person, sometimes with several people, sometimes with a crowd, and sometimes...with no one.

Jesus is always perfect and wise. To be honest, this is an area that I struggle in every day. Who do I give time to? How much time? What should that time look like? I am reminded of the portion of 2 Corinthians that comes immediately before what we have already read today. Let's open our Bibles and read 2 Corinthians 4:11-13.

Name a time you have thrown open your heart to someone and were glad you did so.

Name a time you have thrown open your heart to someone and were burnt.

I have often paid little attention to searching for motives and landed in heartache time and time again. It bites, sisters. *It hurts to land face down on the ground because I went in with my eyes shut and gave everything I had to someone, instead of giving it all to Jesus and letting Him guide the way.* When we open our hearts, there is surely risk. We will get hurt, but if we are consistently hurt, it's time to check our margins, bring them to God in prayer and ask for some wisdom. He gives generously. He does!

Write James 1:5 out in the space below.

Also note that we need different *sizes* of relationship experiences. We need one-on-one conversations and we need group gatherings. Sometimes we even need the crowd. Name one relationship you enjoy one on one.

Name a relationship you enjoy among a group.

Name a crowd or a large gathering where you enjoy the relationships.

We were created for not just supersize – life in the crowd – or mini-size. We were created for all of it...in its time. And sometimes, that means no one but us and God. Rest. A quiet place.

It's hard to speak about boundaries and margins, because just like every other subject, I fail. I'm a sinner, desperately in need of a Savior. But I do know the challenge is worth it. In Christ we are new every day, every moment, thanks to His mercies. We fall down and we get back up, by the strength of His outstretched hand.

Father, help us with our boundaries and our margins. Be in our relationships. Give us clarity and wisdom and love and generosity and Truth and understanding. You, Lord, are perfect and you are perfecting each of us every day, just as we are perfectly holy under Your cross. Help us to live the empty tomb life, outside of shame weighing us down, but honoring you in freedom and in unabashed trust in Your Spirit. In Jesus' name, by which we are saved. Amen.

Exploration
What hard and fast boundaries do you think are important?

In what areas of your life or what relationships are you able to maintain wider margins?

Discuss one person you have a hard time maintaining boundaries with and why. (Feel free to keep the person's name anonymous.)

day five
Another kind of refraining

In looking through the Biblical uses of the word embrace, I came across this passage in Proverbs and felt I would be remiss if we did not address this topic in the space we have here.

Adultery.

It sounds like such a harsh word in our culture. Images of *The Scarlet Letter* come to mind. The word sounds labeling to some people, maybe archaic, and even shaming.

Here is reality:
God cares about sex. He thinks it's a good idea. He created it. He also cares about sex in the boundary of marriage. This is a hard line. Remember yesterday when we discussed boundaries and margins. This is a tight boundary. When I speak about this, please know that it is as a sinner saved by grace alone. I have been, as Paul says, "the worst of sinners." I sit in no place of judgement. But not speaking is not an option. Someone needs to hear the beautiful message of God's good grace.

Sex outside of marriage is dark stuff. It leaves devastation and destruction, fear and regret. Make no mistake, God redeems even this. Of course He does! But the world will tell you that you don't need His redemption. That you do not need Him to stand in that place of forgiveness, after all, our culture tells us it's no big deal.

Hear me now: It is a big deal.

There are always aftershocks. Satan tells us that sex outside of marriage is only between two people. Who can it hurt? Do not be fooled, there are waves of emotional and physical shocks, as well as raw consequences that affect the whole people of God. And God cares...for one sparrow and His entire flock.

Read Proverbs 5:15-23 below, and let's see what wisdom we can glean from the Word, as well as what Grace.

> Drink water from your own cistern,
>   flowing water from your own well.
> Should your springs be scattered abroad,
>   streams of water in the streets?
> Let them be for yourself alone,
>   and not for strangers with you.
> Let your fountain be blessed,
>   and rejoice in the wife of your youth,
>   a lovely deer, a graceful doe.
> Let her breasts fill you at all times with delight;
>   be intoxicated always in her love.
> Why should you be intoxicated, my son,
>   with a forbidden woman
>   and embrace the bosom of an adulteress?
> For a man's ways are before the eyes of the LORD,
>   and he ponders all his paths.
> The iniquities of the wicked ensnare him,
>   and he is held fast in the cords of his sin.
> He dies for lack of discipline,
>   and because of his great folly he is led astray.

This passage is gorgeous. How like God to use such beautiful language to tell us about something the world would degrade so often! He truly is magnificent.

Let's work through the passage just a bit.

First, highlight or underline the first sentence.
"Drink from your own cistern..." Enough said. Not drink from the cistern you have at any given time. Not drink from the cistern that feels right, but drink from the your own cistern, that is your spouse in the one-flesh relationship. And listen for the Gospel...drink from it, friends! Drink deep and share of one another in the marriage bed.

Next highlight or underline the following phrase in Proverbs 5, printed above – "Let them be for yourself alone and not for strangers with you."

Marriage is between two people. Not 3, not 7, but 2 (Mark 10:8). This brings two specific issues to mind.

Privacy
It's important to be sensitive to your partner, no crass joking about your sex life or over-sharing without permission. I'm talking about girl talk around the table too, not just men acting like boys. Be aware of how your partner feels about conversations about sex and use sensitivity.

Pornography
I believe strongly that God has a hard and fast boundary on this one too, and it is demonstrated in this passage. Porn invites other people into your sex life, with or without your partner's permission. It is NOT ok. It is degrading to you, degrading to your spouse, and degrading to the women and men on the screen. It does not build up in any way. Porn is not ok together as a couple, nor is it ok individually – married or single. No matter what age you are, porn messes

with your brain, your future and your current sex life, and your relationship with God. If you have questions about this or need help, please, ask your pastor or visit the ministry of XXX Church at Gospel.com. These are resources of grace and restoration.

Now, highlight the following verses, "...be intoxicated always in her love. Why should you be intoxicated, my son, with a forbidden woman and embrace the bosom of an adulteress?"

God's way of addressing things always strikes me as utterly perfect, usually gentle, always very clear. "Why should you be..."

Yes, why?

God asks us why we would want to give up the abundant life for scraps on the floor. It isn't worth it. Ever. His plans, although a challenge at times, of self-discipline and unclarity, are always better. Always. Why would we embrace the forbidden, when we have the whole garden for ourselves. We trade our relationship of trust with Him and with our spouse or the spouse He has planned for us, for something that falls through our fingers like bathwater from a faucet.

He redeems even that. He redeems all of it. Hold on tight to that.

The Hebrew here offers us special insight, related to our Ecclesiastes study. The verb translated be *intoxicated* in verses 19 and 20 can also be translated *to be led astray* or *to be led far off*. It is so easy to be cast away by another's influence.

But I have Good News. Do you remember where the prodigal was? Luke 15:20 describes the prodigal son was *a long way off*. Cast far away of his own accord. The shame he built around him and heaped on him by his so-called friends created a thick wall. Far off means nothing to God, though. He is the One who removes our sins and breaks down walls. Where does Psalm 103:12 state he removes our sins to?

Far off is speaking God's language. He reaches His hand in the pit of our present or the pit of our past and offers Life.

Life!

There is certainly a time to refrain from embracing. I hope this devotion speaks Life to you and not death and shame. Christ Jesus treasures you. You are precious, beautiful to Him. Shout praises for His ever faithful redemption in the cross and empty tomb. Rest in His bosom. Rest in His Word. Rest in His shelter. When shame and regret press in, when we are called to refrain from embracing in this world, hold fast to Him, embrace the One who loves you more than anything.

Exploration

Have you ever seen the devastating effects of adultery? How were others around the situation affected? (You do not need to be specific.)

What things intoxicate people and create distance between them and God?

How is God Himself intoxicating for our souls, in a good way?

searching, losing,
and being found

Ecclesiastes 3:11a
He has made everything beautiful in its time.

week six
Searching, Losing, and Being Found
Ecclesiastes 3:6

Seeking, searching, and being wholly savable
Losing the lost, a prodigal season
Keeping the younger version of myself
Casting away, a lesson on change
God of the waiting

heart verse:
Let us then with confidence draw near to the throne of grace, that we may receive mercy and find grace to help in time of need.

Hebrews 4:16

day one
Seeking, searching,
and being wholly savable

Let's open to our Ecclesiastes passage first, so we are literally on the same page. Read it in your Bible and then write it out below. Ecclesiastes 3:6 –

Today we're going to seek. :)

Zacchaeus...he was a wee little man. I relate to Zacchaeus, as only another short person can. People my whole life have been identifying for me that I am short. I stand just at 5' 0" tall. Thank you, keepers of all obvious things.

Let's read Zacchaeus' story in Luke 19:1-10. Please, note any interesting facts in the story that stick out to you.

The Bible tells us Zacchaeus was short, not to torture the poor man, but so that we can recognize just how badly he wanted to see Jesus. I have been there. Baptized as a small infant, I had the benefit of the Holy Spirit welling up in me since tininess. I was buried and risen with Christ in the waters.

Like Zacchaeus, I heard about Jesus. I heard He did miraculous things. I heard He cared. I heard He forgave. I am forever grateful to my parents, my pastors, and so many others in my life who walked me through the stories of Scripture and built and planted and tended my faith. I believed and do believe 100%. My problem isn't about believing, but looking.

At some point in young adult life, I realized I believed in Jesus, *but I wanted a closer look*. I wrestled and climbed every tree I could find to see if God was walking down the road on the other side. Doubt for me as a young adult, like so many others, wasn't about losing my faith or walking away. It was about wondering whether I was wholly lovable or even worth the effort. I knew Jesus gave me redemption, a free gift, but could He redeem my past? Could He redeem each sin? Could He redeem all the places where I had stolen, and pretended, and forfeited everything that I claimed to be dear?

I wonder if this is where Zacchaeus was? What do you think? We may not have enough information or insight Biblically, but it is fun to ponder.

Jesus tells us a few really important things about Himself in the account of Zacchaeus. And that's the business we are about – seeking Him.

"I must stay at your house today."
Jesus wants to stay. He wants to stay with Zacchaeus and
He wants to stay with us. We are worth staying with. I don't
have to question it, because He tells me over and over again
in Scripture. Read the following Scripture passages and note
what in each passage reminds you that you are a worthy
place for our Lord to reside – not just to visit, but to *stay*.

Jeremiah 31:2-3

John 17:23

1 John 3:1

2 Corinthians 4:6

Jesus wanted to stay with Zacchaeus not because he was
perfect. Not because he had it all figured out. Zacchaeus
didn't even make any promises for rectifying his untoward
indebtedness until *after* Jesus came to stay with him. Jesus
loved Zacchaeus, He reached out His hand and told him,
"You are worth my time, worth my energy. Let's figure this
out together."

"He has gone to be the guest of a man who is a sinner."
Jesus tells us some things, through His words spoken in this
account, while other things He tells us through the words of
others in the account. These words were all recorded for us.
God-breathed Scripture didn't leave it out for a reason.

"He has gone..."

You can hear the gasping of the Saturday Night Live church
lady. "Sinners??!!"

We should have no patience for pointing and sin-labeling.
Jesus calls it like it is, but He doesn't heap on shame in the
process.

In Matthew 5:46, Jesus tells us with His own words –
> *"For if you love those who love you, what reward do
> you have? Do not even the tax collectors do the
> same?"*

What reward is there in loving those without sin?
Those who fulfill all our desires for us?
Those who never sin against us?
Do these people even exist? No.

Jesus was talking hard stuff here. "Why wouldn't I eat with
sinners?" is Jesus' response throughout Scripture. There is
"reward" in giving to a relationship that isn't perfect. Where
people aren't just giving to you, but you are filling and giving
as well. There will be heartache. Yes. There will be struggle.
Yes. But there will be a life shared, and that is infinitely
better than fake perfection in any relationship.

Jesus, Himself, loves us in our sin. Don't mistake, He doesn't
love sin. He hates it. But He doesn't love me more as I
confess. He loves me the same: yesterday, today, and
tomorrow. We draw closer to Him in our confession and as
we receive absolution.

Chief of sinners though I be...
He loved me in the beginning.
He'll love me at the end.
He loves me in the middle.

"The Son of Man came to seek and save the lost."
Here is the crux of the matter. This is how seeking works.
Jesus—He seeks. He is continually pursuing, sending
people and words into our lives that guide us perpetually
back to Him. He saves us as lost and condemned sinners.
He saves us as we grow and learn throughout our life. He
saves us in our darkest...and in our days full of light.

We seek Jesus because He loves us and that Spirit of Love
rises up in us. When you read these stories of real people in
Scripture, you begin to see and understand and rest in who
Jesus is. You want to know Him more and more and more.
You can't stop seeking Him. It's never enough. John 3:30
says it perfectly. Write that verse out from any translation of
Scripture. If you feel adventurous, write it from two or three
translations for fun.

Because He seeks us, we can be fully confident in ever
seeking Him.

I'll leave you with this week's heart verse, Hebrews 4:16.
> Let us then with confidence draw near to the throne of
> grace, that we may receive mercy and find grace to
> help in time of need.

Approach the throne. Soak in the mercy. Seek some grace.
Embrace the help.

He loves you. Keep seeking. You are fully and wholly found.

Exploration

Take a look at Luke 15. Which one of these "Lost" parables do you most relate to?

Read Luke 15:1 again – who was drawing near to Jesus? Highlight it. Over and over again in Scriptures, He invites people to draw near to Him. What other examples can you remember of Jesus inviting people to draw near to Him?

Tell us about a Bible passage or a person in your life that made you want to know more about Jesus.

day two
Losing the lost, a prodigal season

Today we will piggyback off of Day One, and look more into Luke 15 and the Lost Parables.

First, review Ecclesiastes 3:6.

The word translated as *lose* in the ESV is translated a few different ways by other versions. Look up a few different translations, either using Bibles you have in your home or looking online at a parallel Bible. Write down a few of your findings here:

While many Hebrew scholars would argue for one text being more reliable than another, looking at many of them gives us a good snapshot of what could be chosen from the original Hebrew word.

The essence of the phrase, *a time to lose*, is that there is a time when you had something, and it is now lost to you. There was a time of searching for it even, but that time has passed. There is a time to search no more, to throw your hands in the air and say, "Done."

In yesterday's study we were seeking God. He was seeking us before we could even begin to consider Him. He is a seeking kind of God. But I do not want our desire to understand a pursuing God keep us from understanding the fullness of God. This week we will address again and again the parables of the lost sheep, the lost coin, and the lost son. We'll get to know Luke 15 pretty well, so find a bookmark. When we look at Scripture, God not only gives us a clear message of salvation and the fulfillment of all Law and Gospel, he also gives us pieces of who He is. It's important that we look for that as well when we study the Word.

Let's read Luke 15:15-32. List below all the people who you find that are seeking and who you find have reached "done" at one point or another.

The man and woman in the first two parables do not give up. There is no quitting in these stories. They search and seek until the sheep and the coin are found. In the third parable we get a bigger picture. The third parable helps us to see that there is a time to stop searching. We can reach and seek and search, but sometimes God calls us to stay home and wait, as He Himself has done for each of us.

Have you ever had that relationship with someone? Have you ever felt God speaking to your heart to just stop? To let it be? To leave that work to Him for now? Reflect on this below.

Here is a hard truth that might be a stretch, but worth exploring. There are passages in the Old Testament where our Hebrew word for lose, literally means *to destroy*.

The prodigal Father knew the risks. He knew the heartache at the end of the prodigal road for His son. He loved his son deeply, desperately, but He watched him walk away. He let him walk the path of destruction. He knew that his son may even perish. He metaphorically raised His hands in the air and said, "done" or, maybe more appropriately, "Thy will be done." He let him be lost, but He did not give up on him. He gave him up, so that he could be found.

Sometimes there are those people and relationships and plans and ideas in our lives that God calls us to say "done" to. He does it for a purpose. Don't misunderstand, God's variety of "done" is never uncompassionate. We can pray and ask and seek Him while He works on the details. We will at times experience the pain of heartbreak, we see the one we love, or the plans we held to so tightly, fall into destruction or even perish.

Fear not. We have a God who knows infinitely better than we, who has each of our names written in His book, and Who is waiting on the road. Rest in Him.

Exploration

Have you ever lost something dear to your heart or of value in another way?

Have you ever felt called to say "done" in a search, in a relationship, or with a plan?

How did you do it? How can it be done well? (These things are not mutually exclusive.)

day three

Keeping the younger version of myself

Grace is a living and active part of Christian life. God offers His grace to each of us and to the community of God, in giving His very self by dying on the cross, rising, and placing His Spirit in us. It is so much a part of who He is that we cannot know God without knowing grace.

However, *applying* grace in our lives can be a big challenge.

I am constantly praying for grace. It isn't a justification issue. I know that grace is fully and freely mine in Christ Jesus. I confess and am fully and freely forgiven. I praise and thank Him for the gift of salvation in my life and how that freedom ekes out into every little piece of life lived on this earth.

Rather, it's a sanctification issue. I pray for God to help me let that grace flow out to those around me. That the grace of Christ would wrap itself around my children and my friends, my home, and my community.

We live in a world in need of grace. As a fully redeemed Mama, I want that grace to be in every piece of my parenting, even when it looks like discipline. I want my husband to be engulfed in grace when he walks in the door of our home, instead of me greeting him with "Can you do this? Can you take this? This needs to be done..."

I'm hard on myself about grace, which is ironic in the way that the sanctified life so often is. I'm hard on others when they fail to give me grace. I'm frustrated that grace ends up being something I try to get instead of the free gift given that it really is.

But I'm never more hard on anyone about grace than on my younger self. For years I was actually terrified of my younger self. I wanted so much to remove those years from my memory and never go back. My childhood was great, but if I could only do away with years 13 to about 20, I'd be good to go! 7 years, who would miss them? When God talks about blotting out our sin (Isaiah 43:25), I always assumed He felt the same way. Just blot it out, forget it, no looking back.

At this point you are beginning to wonder what in the world this has to do with Ecclesiastes 3:6. Let's hit refresh on our passage again:

> *a time to seek, and a time to lose;*
> *a time to keep, and a time to cast away;*

There are things we need to keep. There are times we need to keep that maybe we would rather toss away. Seasons that have held sorrow. Seasons that have held rebellion. Seasons that have held something we'd rather wrap up tight in layers upon layers of blankets, encompass with duct tape, and hide in a dark corner of the attic....in someone else's house...that may or may not burn down. Have you ever had a season you'd rather forget? Tell me a little about it here. If it's too painful, feel free to write only a word or phrase and lay it before God in prayer.

Life is wonderful, but also holds its fair share of pain. We are sometimes called to keep, even though there is a cost – a time to keep a friend that holds a bit more drama than we generally care to have in our life, a time to keep a church that we'd rather walk out of so we can go to the church three doors down, a time to keep a marriage that feels like a desert wasteland. Have you ever been called to hold on to a difficult relationship? Share more below if you care to.

Friend, those are all hard things to keep, but sometimes that is what we are called to do. Not always, but sometimes.

For me, I was reminded of my struggle with my younger self when I was driving the other day. I heard a particular song on the radio and the lyrics spoke a hard truth to my heart.

I have always wanted to throw away, to cast away, the younger version of myself. I had no use for that wild and rebellious girl. Any time she came to mind, I could feel the shame rise to my cheeks. Sometimes all it takes is the Spirit knocking at your heart with a verse or lyric.

This time I heard the Gospel loud and clear. Would I do it differently? Yes, maybe, I don't know. I think I always thought grace would be God giving our younger selves a redo. If He would only let my wise-self exist earlier, letting all of it go away, letting a more perfect, more holy version of my youth be the reality is this is what I have learned: God values all of me.

God values all of me.

God would hold me and keep me even through those ugly years. I was, I am, sinful and imperfect but He turns me to Him. He sees the broken as beautiful in light of Christ in my life. I am a piece of precious clay, being molded over time, in relationship with Him. He is ever forming my purpose and giving me Life, as His masterpiece.

Without the younger version of myself, I cannot understand grace.

Am I a sinner now? Yes! But without the growth process, without God working from the inside out, I would only find grace as a nice idea. With it, I *know Grace.* It is the air I breathe, from a Savior who has worked in me from conception, and isn't about to give up on me now.

Let our praises go up! May we keep Him close, just as He keeps every bit of us close to His heart.

searching, losing, and being found

day four
Cast away, a lesson on change

I love throwing stuff away. It's an actual problem. One time I threw away a small pile of bills that Dave had set on the counter to pay. He was not very happy with me and several years down the road, my family still reminds me to "check first, throw away later." Thank you, family. Thank you.

The idea of simplifying, as you can probably tell, speaks to the inner me. What can we get rid of? What around me is piling up and creating internal anxiety, seeping in from my external world? How about you? What in your outer world gives you internal anxiety?

The two stories that comes to mind when I think of the word *casting* are, at first glance, as different as night and day. I think they can help us begin to delve into these questions in our own life: What is God calling me to keep? What is God calling me to cast away?

Keep those two questions in mind as you read today. First, please read Luke 4:31-37. What is being cast away in this passage?

158

Jesus calls us to cast the things out of our lives that are in opposition to Him. Jesus, himself, cast demons out of people because he cared. As the body of Christ-followers, we have the difficult responsibility of helping one another identify and cast out the "demons" in our own lives. Addiction, selfishness, greed, lust, hatred, bitterness, slander, gossip, envy, hurtful words, discontent. This list is not exhaustive. The problem is very complex, this casting off with our neighbor. We constantly need to be doing this in our own life for any of our good intentions with one another to be heard.

Verse 36, above, is not to be missed, *"They were all amazed and said to one another, 'What is this word?'"*

What is this Word? Who is this Jesus? What words of hope from Him do we have to share with one another to cast out the hurt and wounding words, as well as the resentfulness, from one another's lives? Below, write words of hope that come to mind.

When we testify about His Word to one another, this work of casting out is done *together*, in Him.

Second, let's read John 21:1-12. Highlight or underline the word "cast" within this passage in your Bible as you read.

These verses are an invitation to change something up.

The Hebrew word translated *cast away* in Ecclesiastes 3:6b can also be translated *to throw* or *to fling*. It immediately brought to mind the men casting out those nets, throwing them into the water and continuously coming up with nothing. Their hearts were confused after Jesus's death and resurrection, searching for answers, and maybe they just decided to go back to the same ol', same ol', unsure where else to turn.

Many people have this experience in their walk of faith. We know that we have a God who finds, who seeks us, but that doesn't stop us from casting our nets out into the world, searching, hoping, waiting, seeking. While that sounds negative, I don't believe that it necessarily has to be. God has placed that internal desire to seek and search inside of us. We exist in this reciprocal relationship with Him. We live as found people, able to move to the other side of the boat, to throw our nets of fear, and struggle, and doubt into other waters because He is the same God on both sides, and the same Jesus is waiting on the beach to rejoice with us over breakfast at the miraculous catch of His work in our lives.

Praise Jesus! Praise Him! Can you see the nets, stretched taunt with the fish of His faithfulness, His goodness? Be warned, that abundant catch may look a lot more like struggle from the world's perspective. Our catch that we await isn't necessarily a bigger house, or a brand new BFF that adds sunshine and joy to our daily lives. It might be, but in God's economy, it might also be a challenging new ministry opportunity, a new insight that causes us to change something that prunes us, or time spent on a relationship that takes time and energy.

How do we decide when something needs to be cast away or our nets cast into different waters?

We pray. We read His Word.

There is a therapeutic idea called "giving it space." This is when something in life is pressing in – a decision, a relationship, or a discussion. Sometimes we don't have an answer, and God calls us to wait. We can *give it space*. This is taking a moment to give it breathing room. We can stop and pray and seek His word. We needn't press down on the issue and squeeze the life out of it. We can let it sit. God has it in His hands, and He will alert us when the time comes to cast away. And when that time comes, let's do it! Let's be faithful and strong in the Lord by the power of His Spirit.

After all, we're in it together, whether in the waiting or in the casting away...in it together.

Exploration
Are you a keeper, or do you easily throw things away?

What was something you have gotten rid of that you wish you'd kept?

When have you had to change something up in life, and found it wasn't easy?

day five
A God of waiting

To begin today, please read Psalm 27 and choose any two verses to write out below. Which verses speak to you the most?

Why did you choose those two verses?

Now reread Psalm 27:14. Notice in this passage we are introduced to a psalmist who is waiting. I wonder if this psalm is like a pep talk for himself? Or for his men? Is it internal or external dialogue? We don't really know the occasion of the psalm, but we do know that it offers encouragement to the reader in distress and hardship. Matthew Henry's Commentary points out the language of hope in the psalm.

What hope do you hear from the psalmist? What encouragement does it give?

I so often need encouragement in the waiting. Is there someone in your life that you know needs encouragement and hope right now? How could you share this message with them?

Are you in a season of waiting? What are you waiting for?

Sometimes we know and sometimes we do not. Sometimes we can only see the season of waiting in hindsight. We look back and say, "Oh, we were waiting! God was doing His thing and here we are." At other times, we feel stuck in the waiting process. We can literally feel the waiting press in. We are acutely aware of something coming and God's call to wait on Him, to sit with Him for this moment, to be still and wait.

Let's look back at the psalm and work through some verses for greater understanding.

In verse 8, the dialogue between the psalmist and God is gorgeous! God asks us to seek Him, we respond with the heart cry, "Your face, LORD, do I seek." There is assurance in that dialogue. We can return to it over and over again.

Verse 9 has the psalmist pleading *"cast me not off!"* This is a prayer for protection in the waiting. Protection from adversaries, from life's troubles, from loneliness and anxiety. We also can pray for protection. What would you like to ask protection from in this season?

Know that God is holding you in Christ. He does not cast us off.

In verse 10, the author focuses on the promises of God – *"O God of my salvation... [others have forsaken me]... the* LORD *will take me in."*

Have you ever felt forsaken by others?

Have you felt misunderstood?

Have you struggled with where you were placed for a certain time?

God hears your heart and understands. God takes us in through the waters of Baptism and never lets go. He hears us. He never forsakes us.

In verse 13, the author proclaims, *"I will look on the* LORD *in the land of the living..."* Essentially, the psalmist tells us that no matter how this shakes out, we have hope, we can trust, we stand on the solid rock of Eternity.

And finally, verse 14. *"Wait for the* LORD.*"*
I firmly believe that God finds so much value in the waiting. That is so often where His best work is done, in the deep places of our hearts. It takes courage, girls, but we have it in abundance from a Resurrection God.

Do you remember the promise of our Heart verse? *"Let us then with confidence draw near to the throne of grace, that we may receive mercy and find grace to help in time of need."* (Hebrews 4:16)

Let us approach the throne of grace with confidence, find mercy and *help*. Help! We have help!

Keep approaching the throne, whether your season is challenging or ravishing, or wonderfully abundant, or lean and tight, God is in the waiting. He is God of the waiting and He invites us to rest in the waiting.

Exploration
What is the hardest part for you about waiting?

What comes to mind when you picture God sitting on His throne of grace?

What would you like to ask God for help with today?

torn, ripped,
and mended

Ecclesiastes 3:11a
He has made everything beautiful in its time.

week seven
Torn, ripped, and mended
Ecclesiastes 3:7

An opening torn
A God who sews
Foot in mouth, rams horns, and blessed silence
A time to speak or the Great Lunch Boycott of 1996
Mending with words

heart verse
Gracious words are like a honeycomb,
sweetness to the soul
and health to the body.
Proverbs 16:24

torn, ripped, and mended

day one
An opening torn

My friend, Sarah, is a sewer. I am so impressed with her. I do not sew. I can do buttons, or even a patch, but to turn on a machine and create something is not my forte. She creates these beautiful garments, skirts for her goddaughters, fun bags for friends, and very ornate historical costumes. I'm in awe. This week, we'll talk about some sewing.

Let's read our verse for the week to get us started. Write Ecclesiastes 3:7 in the space below.

The word for *tear* in Hebrew is from the root word *qara* (kaw-rah). This word can mean *to tear, to rend, to tear apart, to split apart.* It is often used in the Old Testament in relationship to grief and loss. It sounds like we moved backwards a couple of weeks to revisit weeping and mourning. All over the Old Testament, and even a bit in the New Testament, people are tearing their garments out of grief or distress. Have no fear! While these are commonly related, we are not going to sit there again because we have addressed the concept of grief and mourning already. Let's explore the connection through a few examples.

Read the following passages and answer three questions for each one:
Who is tearing something?
What is being torn?
Why is it being torn?

Genesis 37:29-36 –

Ezra 9:1-9 –

1 Kings 11:7-13 –

In Jesus Christ, God does a different kind of tearing.......a tearing open. That is the tearing we are going to look at today. There is a time for tearing in response to grief and loss, but here we see that God has revealed something new. He has torn the Old away and ushered in the New. Let's look at Matthew 27:45-54. What is torn in this passage?

The new has come.

With Christ's death on the cross, everything holy is open wide. Doors flung open, *torn* open. The tearing is painful, but Christ took that tearing for you and for me. And when that temple curtain was torn in two and opened wide, forgiveness and mercy came in a way the world had not been even capable of considering before.

Read Hebrews 10:14-23 for further understanding. Look through the passage and find these phrases:
> *...a single offering...*
> *...the Holy Spirit also bears witness...*
> *...the covenant that I will make...*
> *Where there is forgiveness...*
> *...the new and living way...*
> *...full assurance of faith...*

He who promised is faithful. All I can say to that is *Amen!* Which one of these phrases speaks Grace into your life this day? Can you breath it in? These words feel fresh off the page to me as I write this, even though they are centuries old. Spend a few more moments in Hebrews 10 and bask in the mercy of the New Covenant.

Fill in the blanks of Hebrews 10:19-20 –
> *"Therefore, brothers, since we have* _____
>
> *to enter the* _____ _____ _____
>
> *by the blood of Jesus, by the new and living way that*
>
> *he opened for us* _____ _____
>
> _____, *that is, through his flesh..."*

He has opened the holy places for us. The curtain torn in two means that we no longer need to rend anything. Turn to Joel 2:12-13; note the who, what, and why of tearing in these verses. This call to repentance before God reminds us that we have traded in our tearing for something far better. List the attributes of God mentioned in Joel. We now enjoy this new kind of freedom in relationship with Him because of Christ Jesus.

The message of Scripture within the framework of Christ's new covenant for us as believers is *Christ opens hearts.*

Christ opens up unhindered relationship, for us, with God.

We can *"draw near with a true heart in full assurance..."* We stand before God and ask Him to open wide our hearts. Open wide our hearts to Him, to His children, to His work, to everything that is eternal and gracious and just.

When we read the word *tear* in Scripture, because of Christ's death in our place, we can boldly ask God to tear open anything that stands between Him and ourselves. He has already torn down all barriers once and for all. In Christ, we stand assured. He is faithful.

Father, we thank You for Your work in our lives. We thank You for Your death and resurrection. We thank you for offering yourself. Yourself, for us. We lay our hearts before you, praising you. Asking you to keep working on us. To keep us firm in the knowledge of your continual work in our lives. In Jesus' name we pray, Amen.

175

Exploration

What expressions of grief have you seen or experienced that were helpful in mourning?

What Old Testament stories do you remember about the Temple?

What has God opened your heart to over time and what do you think He is asking you to open your heart to currently?

torn, ripped,
and mended

day two
A God who sews

I have orange pants. They are skinny corduroys. I love my orange pants.

I love them so much that I brought them to Haiti with me...in August. Anyone who has even had any experience in subtropical climates knows how ridiculous this is. But I love the pants and couldn't bear to just leave them in a drawer at home. Ridiculous.

I have sewn these pants. They got a weird tear by the zipper and they were easily fixed with a needle and some tough thread. Then there was a small rip in the bottom near the seam, so I stitched that up. After doing the laundry, Sunday, I noticed a new rip near the zipper, so now they set in a prominent place on my dresser, as a reminder to "fix me." Some pants are worth fixing, you know?

Some things in life are worth sewing.

Our God is a God that recognizes the value of sewing, the value of mending.

The earliest act of sewing we can find is in Genesis 3:7-13. What was the first item sewn and why?

Adam and Eve first sewed to cover their shame. They had sinned against the God that they walked with in the garden. They had dishonored themselves and all that He had given them in their unbelief. The serpent planted distrust, "Did God really say..." and they tossed aside Who they knew Him to be, for who they let the devil tell them He was. God responds with a whole host of discipline in Genesis 3, but what does Proverbs 3:12 offer us as a reminder of His goodness?

He also gives us a glimpse of the Gospel in Genesis 3:15. Yes, the serpent will nip at Christ's heel in Jesus's death and resurrection, but Christ will crush the serpent's head in the victory that the cross brings. In the Garden, He poured the Gospel out onto His precious children in Genesis 3:21. Write that passage below.

What grace does God offer Adam and Eve in this passage?

One of the earliest records of God's actions for His people is of God sewing. It makes me tear up to think of a God who looks at Adam and Eve's paltry cover for the shame of their sin and says, "Let me lift that. Let me cover you with my garment." God, in His earliest acts of love takes off our garment of shame and replaces it with sacrifices for us. It astounds me. His love is unfathomable. Beautiful.

God continues to weave this part of His character throughout His Word. Find encouragement as you read the words of Isaiah 61:10 and Psalm 30:10-12. What do each of these verses tell us about what God has clothed us with?

When we flip forward to the Gospel accounts in Matthew, Mark, Luke, and John, we read a different story about clothing.

Jesus Christ was stripped naked and put on a cross; He bore the utmost shame, to lift ours.

Let your head be lifted, friend. What did you put on today? We wear clothing, be it orange pants or maxi skirts, or sackcloth, because of sin. We cover the intimate places, because we all have darkness inside of us. But this is not where we live now. We are clothed by a Savior who loves us, who gives us His garments of righteousness and purity and holiness. He also gives us what we need daily, and sometimes that looks like really fun pants. Those pants can just be fun, or they can also remind us of Who He is – a God who loves us enough to cover us, lift us, and provide for us.

When you get dressed or undressed today, thank a God who sews. Thank a God who cares intimately about every little thing. Honor Him, love Him. He loved you first.

Exploration

What is your favorite article of clothing that you currently own, or that you have ever owned?

Do you sew or know anyone who sews? Tell us about that. What mechanics of sewing come to mind to serve as reminders of God's tender care in our lives?

What shame has God lifted from your life and borne for you? What has He replaced that shame with – forgiveness, joy, mercy, etc.? What burden has this lifted from you?

torn, ripped, and mended

day three
Foot in mouth, rams horns, and blessed silence

Keeping silent is not in my nature. It is not necessarily opposed to my nature, but we all have things God asks of us that are a tad harder. This is mine. Patience, gentleness, and silence. These are my challenges.

One time in college, one of my professors turned to me and said, "I want you to count to ten before you answer a question in this class. Let's just see if anyone else answers first. Just wait and see." She was speaking the truth in love, for sure, and at the time, as hard as it was to hear, these words of truth cut to my heart and change began. To this day, I usually count to ten before answering anything in a group situation. And I still praise God for that admonishment to grow up. I didn't get it instantly, but I got it eventually. And I'm still a work in progress.

God tells us there is indeed a time to keep silence. Write out Ecclesiastes 3:7 below, to bring it to the front of your thoughts today.

I love the language of the ESV translation – holding silence is a precious commodity. In a world filled with noise, we have the opportunity, the gift from God, to hold silence close.

The Hebrew root word for silence in Ecclesiastes 3:7, *chashah*, is an active word. This kind of silence is not simply silent because there is a lack of noise, but rather silence has been chosen.

Most of us, as siblings, moms, or grandmas understand the value of silence. In a house full of small people, I try to teach the value of silence every day. My children, like myself, love to fill the void. Noise, laughter, arguing, and daily living all compete with silence. And there is a time for these things. The back and forth, the seasons and cycles of life, are all a part of the essence of Ecclesiastes 3.

What else does God have to say about the value of silence?

Joshua 6 contains a fun story many of us remember from our youth – Joshua and the Battle of Jericho. Let's read it together and see how God worked in the silence and in the shouting.

Read Joshua 6:8-16 and focus in on verse 10.

Joshua 6:10 tells us that the people were instructed not to shout or open their mouth until they were instructed to do so. These instructions may seem odd to us, even contrary to our nature, but God has a plan. Many times God works in the silence. When we seize the opportunity to hold our tongues in a stressful situation in particular, we let God do His work instead of getting in the way. God may call on us to speak, just as on the seventh day the Israelites shouted, but the time in between can be used to seek God, to pray for the words, to be given wisdom and insight.

Jesus took many opportunities to remain silent. What does Isaiah 53:7 tell us about the Lamb of God?

It's beautiful! Perhaps one of the stories where Jesus' intentional silence is the most clear is found in Matthew 27:11-14, when Jesus comes before Pilate. Read this passage from Matthew's Gospel. Jesus keeps silence in this passage two times. List both instances below.

Why does Jesus avoid answering, or rather, why does Jesus intentionally keep silence? I don't know, but what we do know is that God always has a plan and Jesus is always walking in and through that plan, not looking to skirt around it. He chose silence and left Pilate amazed.

I discovered another beautiful verse at a time in my life when silence was my only option. When life itself had taken away my speech, when I was world weary, trampled on, and exhausted from the battle of it all. Have you ever had a time in your life when you were at a loss for words because life was hard?

Our next passage is a balm for the soul in times when we have no words.

Read Exodus 14:13-14, and write out verse 14 below.

Sometimes the battle is truly not ours; it is God's. He would have us hand it to Him and let Him do what He does best.

A time to keep silence sounds restful to me. I pray today that you find some rest in God, a moment to be silent in His presence with His Word. *You speak, Lord, and we'll be silent for a moment. We're listening.*

Exploration
Are you a talkative person or quieter by nature?

Have you ever stuck your foot in your mouth, so to speak?

When have you been blessed by a period of silence and rest?

torn, ripped,
and mended

day four
A time to speak
or the Great Lunch Boycott of 1996

I really enjoy a good protest. Not unnecessary protest, mind you, but there is so much joy in standing up for something you believe in. I feel blessed to be a part of that process.

When I was a junior in high school I was involved in my first large group protest. It was a quiet but mighty protest, which strikes me as one of the best kinds. And it all started around a school lunch table.

When I was in high school, there were squares on a lunch tray. You could fill your tray from the small selection of items, or you could bring your lunch. This worked for me most of the time, until the day I wanted an apple.

Apples, yum! Who doesn't love 'em?! An apple was $1.00, or I could walk three feet to the right and buy a Snickers bar for $.50 at the student council store...decisions, decisions. You can guess the terrible health decisions that occurred based on this ridiculousness. I looked around me. What if you had limited funds or little access to good food otherwise? I became incensed. So did a few of my other lunch table cohorts and the wheels of change began to turn for a handful of high school students.

We organized a large and successful lunch boycott. This was so life changing for me, stepping up, in a massive way, and refusing to overlook injustice (no matter how small), that I wrote about it in my entrance essay for graduate school. My social-work-self relished that moment when my principal called us into his office and said, "Shut down the boycott, or you'll find yourselves suspended." You can imagine our response.

After another week of the growing boycott, "You'll get suspended" turned into "what do you want?"

"I want a world where apples are served in one of my squares, without costing more than carbohydrates. I want edible green stuff on another square. I want Thanksgiving lunch more than once a year. I want a salad bar."

Our words and requests weren't really about food. What they really said was, "I want to be listened to. I want to be valued. I want my opinion to not just be tolerated, but to have an impact."

We have a God who says, "Yes! You are worth listening to. You are valued. Your opinion matters. You have an eternal impact."

And about things that matter so much more than what sits on my lunch tray...
Topics like
    abortion
    destructive sexual relationships
    abuse
    human trafficking
    poverty
    prejudice
    hatred

Please add any topics to the list above that come to mind for you.

God's work is done when we bring light to the dark places, and so often that means speaking up, speaking out, and speaking with.

What does Proverbs 31:8-9 instruct us to do?

Who especially needs your voice right now?

Look at Ephesians 4:15. What exhortation for speech is given in this verse?

Look at the following verses. Identify beside each reference when and for whom we are given charge to speak up.

Psalm 82:3

Isaiah 1:17

Zechariah 7:9-10

All these verses ask us to stand against oppression, stand against the darkness, and speak for justice. We know that we can speak up for others, because we have someone who pleads for us every day – Jesus Christ. He intercedes for us, forgives us, and renews us for every good work. He is the voice of the voiceless in the heavenly places, so that we may sing His sweet praise.

Lord, speak through your children. Use me. Direct me. Mold me to ever speak Your Truth in love to Your people. In Jesus' name we pray, Amen.

Exploration
What topic is important enough to make you break silence?

What avenues do you think go unnoticed when it is time to speak up?

What pitfalls and benefits come with speaking up on social media?

torn, ripped, and mended

day five
Mending with words

Our words matter. We know it in our heads. We just have a hard time making the transfer from knowing this to living life according to that knowledge.

The Bible speaks all kinds of Truth about our words which we would be wise to heed. It also speaks grace over every single area we live. Jesus lived perfectly so because we can't. But He is working on me, every day, every hour, perfecting and teaching, until the day I see His face and know in full (1 Corinthians 13:12).

Today, I want you to hear the truth held out for us in Proverbs 16:18-25. What words or phrases do you notice that offer wisdom for our words?

For today, let's zero in on three specific pieces of wisdom found in these verses:

Pride leads to destruction. *Proverbs 16:18*

Pride will always hurt ourselves and our relationships. Things spoken with pride, even when it is not intended, chip away and destroy others bit by bit. Paul recommends that when we boast we boast in the Lord, not ourselves, not our children, not our ethnic group, not our class, or any of that.

This sounds kind of harsh, but picture it this way...what areas of life are taken up by our pride, rather than speaking Life and Jesus? Even when I hop on Facebook to tell everyone how awesome my life and my 4 kids are, how can I shape my words to give glory to Him, honestly, authentically, instead of myself, or even my little ones?

A wise heart uses judicious speech, sweet speech, discernment, and persuasiveness. *Proverbs 16:21,23*

Note that persuasiveness is different than manipulative speech. Persuasive speech that is also discerning is concerned with what God thinks of things. It doesn't persuade for the sake of the speaker, but persuades because of the value placed on the individual they are speaking to by a loving God.

What in the world is judicious? It is speech that has good judgement and sense. It has good timing and concern for the listener. It is sensitive to a person's culture, maturity, and life situation. It is sweet and gentle. It is kind. The question here is "How can the person I am speaking with *best understand* the message I am sending?" Not "I must get them to understand my message come what may!" Sometimes the words that seem right do not speak Life, and Jesus is always Life. (v. 25)

Gracious words are like honeycomb, sweetness to the soul, health to the body. *Proverbs 16:24*

I could be accused of taking this verse too literally, but listen to the Life wrapped around them. Research shows that children who have been abused and/or neglected are more likely to have chronic illnesses, asthma, colds, and reduced immunity. Abusive words are often cited by survivors of abuse as the worst part. Words can bring Life and health or death and destruction.

Jesus speaks health and sweetness into our lives with His Word. He tells us we are loved, we are chosen, we are valued, we are forgiven, we are free. He also tells us that we are in need of forgiveness, that we do mess up, that our life without him resembles a pit; even that is balm to the soul when you know a God who runs down the road, reaches into the pit Himself, and lifts your head up to His praise and honor. Our words of grace and truth are worth speaking to those around us, to a hurting world, desperate for the honeycomb of Christ Jesus.

Today, we pray especially for our homes, where so many of our words are exchanged. Lord, you fill us up and tend to our every need. May Your Words flow out of us at the proper time in all Grace and Truth. Use us, Lord. Give us Your wisdom. We stand as vessels; empty us of ourselves and fill us with the Sweetness of Your Spirit. In Jesus' name we pray, Amen.

Exploration
When was a time that someone's sweet words gave you health and life?

What are some of your favorite words of sweetness in Scripture?

Share one challenge you can identify in sharing Truth as well as Grace in your cultural context.

peace, love,
and war

week eight

Peace, love, and war
Ecclesiastes 3:8

People are always worth it: A time to love
The ugly H-word
Wars and rumors of wars
But now in Christ...
Searching for mommy-peace

heart verse

*In overflowing anger for a moment
I hid my face from you,
but with everlasting love I will have
compassion on you,"
says the LORD, your Redeemer.
Isaiah 54:8*

peace, love, and war

day one
People are always worth it: A time to love

The Bible is full of real and fun accounts of love. I am reminded of one youth night. We had our Bibles open to the story of Isaac and Rebekah and my husband, who is ever wonderful and goofy, stood up and proclaimed dramatically, "Pay attention! This is the one with love at first sight." He then proceeded to act out the entire story as a one man show, with sweeping arm gestures. We were all in stitches, and if you open to Genesis 24, you'll see why. Skim through the chapter and note how many times the word *behold* is used. Now look particularly at the intensity of Isaac and Rebekah's eyes meeting in verses 63-67. Fill in the missing words of Genesis 24:67 below:

> *Then Isaac brought her into the tent of Sarah his*
>
> *mother and took Rebekah, and she became his wife,*
>
> *and _____ _____ _____.*
>
> *So Isaac was comforted after his mother's death.*

It's so sweet and, most importantly, so real.

There are many more stories of romantic love, both beautiful and painful, in the Bible.

We also see real friendship love in Biblical relationships, as well as the love God has for individuals and His people as a whole. Look up the following Scripture texts and note which individuals are involved and what kind of love is expressed and shown or what kind of love is lacking –

Genesis 29:18

Genesis 29:30, 32-34

1 Samuel 1:1-2, 7-8

1 Samuel 18:1-3

John 13:23

1 John 3:1

Isaiah 54:8

Romans 8:38-39

Whether considered as an objective thing or as an emotion, love is not optional. It is a gift from the Father, given with and through the Son and the Spirit. We were designed to receive it and to give it. We cannot live without it. We need it like we need air and water. It is the sustenance of life.

What is the first and greatest commandment? Read Matthew 22:37-40 to answer this question.

What is the second commandment according to Jesus?

We were designed for love. It's a Biblical Truth.

In our Ecclesiastes passage this week, there are three little words in front of love that change our discussion a bit. Let's look and see. Read Ecclesiastes 3:8, and fill in the blanks below.

_____ _____ _____ *love, and a time to hate;*
a time for war, and a time for peace.

A time to love would insinuate that there is a time *not* to love, and indeed if we look at Ecclesiastes 3:8 further, there is, in fact, a time to hate.

Let's consider this for a moment. We know Jesus, so we are always filled with His love and always called to love. This is our Biblical Truth. The difference is that the action of love may look a whole lot different than we expect in any given season of our lives and relationships.

Read 1 John 4:8 below and underline or highlight the last three words of the verse.

> *Anyone who does not love does not know God, because God is love.*

His Spirit lives in us, as baptized believers, so we are never without love. Living in a season without love is just not our New Testament reality. But our *experience and expressions* of love in life may not look like the world's understanding of love.

There will be times in even a life filled to the brim with God's love when we feel lonely. There will be times when we feel lost and sad and left behind. There will also be times when we will be called to love in a way that looks a whole lot like expressed anger and frustration, or a removal of time and energy in a relationship. Our experience of love may look a lot like "a time to love, a time to hate" woven together. Not in a willy-nilly, haphazard throwing around of emotions, but a casting out and pulling in of relationship in order to care for those who need to be cared for at any given time. By setting boundaries and speaking the truth in love, we share life in a real and legitimate way, instead of an inauthentic love that reeks of flowers and chocolate but destructive behavior.

It's exhausting to discern. Relationships always are. But we have an inexhaustible God, who lives in us, and frees us for the challenge.

I was telling a tale of relational woe and difficult relationships to a friend the other day and her words stopped me in my tracks, "Well, it's like you always say...'People are always worth it.'"

I didn't even know I always say that! But evidently I do. And there's a reason:

People are always worth it.

In this life, that is the dance of love and hate, struggle and joy, seeking and receiving. During our short little time here on earth, people are always God's primary concern, and so they will be mine.

Through the pain and sorrow of figuring out relationships, to the sharing of love by hugging and laughing, or acknowledging and toppling idols in one another's lives, I'm all in. I'm not going to be halfway in, protecting a corner of my heart where no one gets in. I have an all-in Savior, with an all-in love.

Isaiah 54:8 from earlier speaks the truth of this in our lives...
"In overflowing anger for a moment
I hid my face from you,
but with everlasting love I will have
compassion on you,"
says the LORD, your Redeemer.

Love poured out in a face hidden. This may look so different than something we would normally label as love, but it doesn't change the truth of it.

It's a challenge, but I promise you – People are always worth it.

Exploration

When have you been forced to express love in a different kind of way?

Has God ever taken you through a season of loneliness or sadness to show you the depth of His love?

Where are the dark places you can show love? (Think about issues like abortion and human trafficking, or individual relationships like speaking up against someone's affair.)

What are other alternative expressions of love that you can think of, that the world would deem unloving or even hateful?

peace, love, and war

day two
The ugly H-word

Hate is not my favorite word. I hold strongly to the general mom-ism that scolds, "We don't say hate. You may strongly dislike something, but you don't hate it." Granted, in our house, we are almost always talking about what's for dinner, but still, *hate* is a strong word. I fight hard to convince my children to think through their words and use them well.

How does my mom-self make peace with the fact that the ESV translation of the Bible uses the word *hate* 169 times? How do I explain to my children that there are in fact times to hate according to Ecclesiastes 3:8? Open your Bible and review this passage for yourself.

Yesterday's study was pretty abstract, so let's try to get down to some practical nuts and bolts in today's study. Just like yesterday, though, we can only understand love and hate through laying out what lies in Truth and what lies in our experiences.

First, hate is sometimes an expression between people.
Most of the time, when the Bible uses the word *hate*, it is
used as a human expression between two people. This kind
of hate is always outside of God's will for us. Look again at
the story of Jacob and Leah from yesterday. Read Genesis
29:21-31. What trouble does hate stir up in this passage?

The Bible does not mince words. What were Jacob's feelings
toward Leah and how does God respond to her need for love
and affection?

Joseph also was hated by his brothers. Many people
expressed hatred toward Jesus, which pushed forward His
death. People across time, from political leaders to
neighbors across lawns, have hated and harmed one
another. This is not our God at work in us. What comes to
mind for you when you think of the destruction of hate across
time and history?

Where is God in all of this? Read the promise God gives us
in trouble and hate, through Joshua 1:9.

In the Bible, sometimes hate is directed at God.
Deuteronomy 5 instructs us that there are two responses in
our relationship with God. We can love God with our whole
heart, soul, mind, and strength, or we can hate Him. There's
no lukewarm in God's economy. Read Deuteronomy 5:8-10
and note which commandment encompasses this.

God does hate some *things*.

Again, Deuteronomy says it super-clearly. Flip forward to Deuteronomy 16:22. What does this passage reveal to us that God hates?

A pillar is an idol. God hates idols. They steal us from him, and if you remember from yesterday's study, sometimes we are called to help others topple their idols. Sometimes, we need to let others in to help topple our own. This doesn't always look like love to the world, but it is.

What else does God hate? Read Psalm 11:5 and Proverbs 6:16-19 and list some of the things you discover from these passages that God hates.

Wickedness and violence afflicted on His people, on His children...He hates it. Why? Because it hurts. Hurtful words are not ok. Plots and plans against anyone, He hates it. In this we can see that God's hate is still driven by love.

God calls us to hate some things, but only so we can fully love.

I think one of the most fascinating and difficult passages of Scripture can be found in Luke 14:26:

> *If anyone comes to me and does not hate his own father and mother and wife and children and brothers and sisters, yes, and even his own life, he cannot be my disciple.*

For a fuller context, you can also read the parables that Jesus teaches throughout Luke 14. For our time here, we'll put this statement in the context of Scripture as a whole.

Jesus wants all of us.

What parts of us does He want according to Mark 12:30?

This message crosses the Old and New Covenants as God instructs His people in Deuteronomy and then *puts Himself in us to make it a reality at Pentecost*. What a God we have!

Jesus wants us to lose our life, to lose putting relationships and people and things and plans ahead of Him, so that we can gain everything, which *is* Him. He uses the strong word *hate* in Luke 24 because it's black and white. "Me or the other stuff," He says.

We hate the idea of anything – mother, brother, friend, job, children, even church – being more than Him in our lives. When we cling fast to Him in the Spirit, we will know boundless love that we cannot even imagine, far more than enough for all our earthly relationships.

There is a practical application to this. We can love God and fill our life with stuff and people and crazy amounts of love. We can even love the stuff and the people more than God and still be saved. We'll go to heaven, we aren't less of a believer, but what we will be missing is the abundant life, the surrendered life, for sure. And it's a mighty fine line.

Jesus gave us all of Himself. Because Jesus gave me all of Himself, I can give Him all of me.

Jesus tells us that this is better than giving part to Him and part to my family and friends and the stuff of life. When He has all of me, He fills in all the blanks because I've handed it all to Him. He loves my mother and my brother and my neighbor through me, and that is infinitely better than I could ever do on my own.

Let Him love. Let Him take over all of you. Let Him fill in all the crevices and relationships so that the people in your life can be truly loved without limits.

This means we say no to some things. This means we may move away, or spend our holiday differently than our family prefers. This means we may chose a God-plan that no one likes, or share a Gospel that no one wants to hear. It may make for difficult relationships on this earth...but eternity together.

So it's probably time for me to make a little peace with the word hate. It sounds ugly, but God makes the ugly beautiful in His time. I'm going to hate what isn't Him, so that He can fill in those dark places with His Light.

Placing it all into His loving care.

Lord, help us to love You with our whole hearts and to let Your Spirit well up in us and guide us and lead us. In You, Lord, there is Peace and Life, Truth and true Love. In Jesus' name we pray. Amen.

Exploration

Have you ever had a relationship made difficult by your belief in Jesus?

How do you share Jesus with those in your family (or friends) who do not know Him?

Who can we pray for in your life that they may come to know Jesus's love for them?

peace, love, and war

day three
Wars and rumors of wars

The idea of war is pretty frightening to me. I am blessed to have grown up in a generation without war. Desert Storm has been the most heated conflict in my lifetime thus far. As a child, I heard stories of World War I and World War II, Vietnam and Korea, but they seemed distant from my life in a peaceful country. The possibility for war came crashing in with the Iraqi conflict. That year, I remember going on vacation and coming back to sluggish brown water coming out of our taps. I was 12 and terrified that chemical warfare had arrived on our doorstep. My mom spent hours of her life soothing me with the lesson that a backup of minerals in our faucets and pipes after a long break can cause tinted water for a short time. Whew. I could sleep again.

What about war is at the heart of my fears...or dare I say *our* fears? I know I'm not the only one. War is scary stuff. Killing, destruction, domination, fighting...all these words come to mind when I think of war. What comes to your mind? This may be an anxiety-producing exercise, but I think it's worth examining. We need to be able to sit with the reality for just a little, in order for it to lose its grip on us. War is and will be a reality on this Earth, even when political peace reigns for a time. List words that come to mind when you think of war.

Ecclesiastes 3:8 reminds us that there will be *a time for war, a time for peace.*

Jesus also instructs us to be realistic in Matthew 24:1-13. It's not a cheerful passage, but it is Truth. And we can remind ourselves of Who is speaking as we read it. He is an all-powerful Savior. Picture Him speaking directly to you as you read this passage in Matthew.

How is it possible that, as Christians, we can praise the Lord even for this, for war?

We live with one foot in one world and one foot in another. I remember, on our honeymoon, we visited the Four Corners region. Every tourist was chomping at the bit, myself included, to have their picture taken with their feet in two "places" at once. We already live in two places every day! We live as eternal people, given eternal life now. We have one foot planted in the reaches of eternity, where time is endless, tears cease, and peace reigns. We are still called to live here, where fighting and wars are real, where people hurt and give pain. Both Ecclesiastes and Jesus's words in Matthew remind us that all this junk is purposeful. It leads us *to* something...namely, Him.

There will be a time when we live with two feet firmly planted on completely restored soil. Our bodies will be whole and perfect. Our hearts and minds will be linked inexplicably with Him, in a way that right now we only know in part.
The beauty of studying the Hebrew language in a passage is that we begin to see a little more of the fullness of God's Word. I found two passages that I can't wait to share. They employ the same Hebrew root as the word for *war* in Ecclesiastes 3:8. Bask in the beauty of it with me. Circle each reference to war and battle you find in each translation of the passages.

Exodus 15:3 –
> *The Lord is a man of war;*
>> *the Lord is his name. (ESV)*

> *The Lord is a warrior;*
>> *the Lord is his name. (NIV)*

Psalm 24:8 –
> *Who is this King of glory?*
>> *The Lord, strong and mighty,*
>> *the Lord, mighty in battle! (ESV)*

> *Who is the King of glory?*
>> *The Lord, strong and mighty;*
>> *the Lord, invincible in battle. (NLT)*

The Lord! The Lord is a warrior. He is mighty in battle. All the wars and rumors of wars that swirl around us – they are nothing to the victory that will be God's Son revealed in majesty at the Restoration. He is so Good!

There is a time for war. The Bible tells us so, as much as we'd like to escape it. God tells us it is purposeful. It brings Him – in the flesh, reigning forever – that much closer to us. Until then, we fight daily in the battle against Satan for the dear souls of those we love around us. The Spirit is our strong soldier, but the devil just doesn't let up. Neither does our Savior, and He has a secret that Satan knows but won't accept – He's already won the victory.

I'm looking forward to that two-feet-in-one-place day. Imagine it! Until then...we're standing in the victory together. When anxiety threatens, remember: the time for war—even this!—is in His hands.

Exploration
What conflicts, wars, and threats of wars do you remember in your lifetime?

What do you think the scariest part of war is for people?

How does knowing Jesus has already won the victory make the reality of war a different thing for us?

peace, love, and war

day four
But now in Christ...

Peace is something we don't necessarily notice until it's gone. It's easy to take for granted, until it dissipates in a moment.

My husband told the story, in a recent sermon, of Horatio G. Spafford. Mr. Spafford was a businessman that put pen to paper to express his sorrow and trust through the hymn, "It is Well." His story is heart wrenching, but when you sing it, knowing the life behind the song gives it so much more depth and richness. Every person has a life, every hymn writer, every pastor, every businessman, every fast food worker, every unemployed anyone, every single one of us. Every person has a story, and in taking time to hear it, we also hear God's work, in the darkness and in the joy.

Mr. Spafford, after losing his fortune and his son, sent his 4 daughters and wife to Europe for a time of relaxation and rest after struggle. He was to join them, but was detained by business and forced to take a later boat. The boat holding his heart – his wife and daughters – was struck and sunk in a matter of minutes. His wife survived. All of his daughters drowned.

Can you even imagine? As he traveled across the sea to meet his wife, he penned the words to "It Is Well."
> When peace, like a river, attendeth my way,
> When sorrows like sea billows roll;
> Whatever my lot, Thou hast taught me to say,
> It is well, it is well with my soul. (Public domain)

One thing I have learned from Mr. Spafford is this: a time for peace does not always look like peace to the world around us. As Christians, we know this with certainty. Let's solidify it in the Word.

The Hebrew word for *peace* in Ecclesiastes 3:8 is probably familiar – *shalom.* In other places in Scripture it is also translated as *be at ease* (Genesis 43:23) and, wouldn't you know it – *it is well.*

We know where our peace lies – securely in Jesus. And He never changes. Look at Gideon's experience in Judges 6:23-24. How does God assure Gideon that God offers something different from the world?

Isaiah 9:6 tells us that the very name of God is peace. List the names for God found in this single verse of Scripture.

The incarnation of Jesus Christ and the residence of His Holy Spirit in our hearts brings *a time for peace* into any situation! What assurance!

This truth is perhaps most evident in Ephesians 2:13-14. Note the first four words of the passage by writing them below.

This is what Mr. Spafford knew. This is what we know and learn and grow in, as God does His work in our lives and hearts.

But now in Christ, we have peace in our hearts.

But now in Christ, we rest in Him. But now in Christ, with the victory won, we trust that all of it – the good, the bad, the dark, the light, the love, the hate, the war, and the peace – will work together for the good of those that love God (Romans 8:28).

Shalom, sisters. Take a deep breath, in and out. Peace lives in you. Now is your time for peace in Christ.

Exploration
When do you find it most difficult to concretely feel at peace?

What do you do or where do you go when you are in need of physical, mental, or emotional peace?

Who could use a reminder of God's *shalom*, God's peace today? Who needs the reminder of an unchanging God, who is always with us?

peace, love, and war

day five
Searching for mommy-peace

Peace is a word that seems to elude me. I love standing in the truth of peace in Christ, because on any given day, my world is not so peaceful. It is simply not my season.

The snapshot of my life looks like a lot of rushing, a lot of gathering, a lot of cajoling into socks and underwear, small people who would rather streak naked through the church parking lot outside of my house to get to the playground on the other side. It looks like hurried breakfasts and sneakers put on in the car. It looks like wading through papers to find the one I lost, and verbalizing my angst that people use hard copies made of paper anymore. It looks like worry over educational choices for my children, worry over whether my husband's message will be well-received, and worry about whether we're weird enough to be cool-weird, or just weird enough to be abnormal.

I can hear Jesus in my ear, His gentle voice laughingly telling me, "Why do you worry, My Precious One? Why so rushed? Why so unsettled?"

For a time I can settle down. I can sit in His Word at His feet. It's why Bible study is my lifeblood. It's my I.V. of sanity in a world that feels so out of control, reminding me of His true and steadfast peace.

As we near the end of our study of Ecclesiastes, and wrap up these verses marked *a time for this...a time for that*, I'm reminded of all the wise women who have sat next to me. Each of them at some time stated absently "These days won't last forever. Treasure them. Hold on to them tightly." I can hear my mom's voice, "this too shall pass." These busy days won't be forever.

You do not have to be in the middle of mommy-struggles to understand the truth of those words. Experience in this instance, however, is a good teacher. As you age – whether into new adulthood or further down the road – you become ever more aware that years happen more in blinks than as slow-moving locomotives.

If there is anything to be learned from Ecclesiastes 3:1-8, let it be this: There is a time for everything. Which also means that there is a time for *each thing*...and that each season, each thing will pass. We will spend our whole lives saying goodbye to things in whooshes as they sojourn with us for a moment and then pass us by.

Remember the day you started middle school and thought it would never be over? Remember the days of sorrow over a first love lost? Those days felt eternal, like you would never be happy again. Do you have any childhood memories of summers of joy and freedom and star-filled nights and crickets, when the clock moved too quickly and too slowly all at once? Maybe you remember college dorms, and cafeteria food, and discount tickets to ball games, and holing up in your cubby in the library until they kicked you out, and girl-talk on someone's loft bed? Maybe you remember the first years of marriage, sweet dates of grilled cheese and movies on the living room floor, buying a coffee maker, just because that's what adults do, and finding out that not everyone makes their bed and you just committed your life to one of them. Are any of these memories speaking to you? Share a memory of your own. What sweet memories come to mind of a time that has passed by?

Read back through Ecclesiastes 3:1-8 in its entirety. What great graces has Our Lord bestowed on you in your days? What carefree days has God blessed you with? What days saddled with responsibility has He seen you through in faithfulness? What precious days or memories and moments has he woven into the fabric of your story? Make a small list below of names or places or words that belong to your story.

Thank Him for every single piece of it.
Breathe in and breathe out.
Let His Spirit move in you and let it rise up to pray,
You, God, are glorious! You send the sun to mark day, and the moon to mark each night. As each day passes, Lord, we praise You for Who You are and what You are doing in every moment of our lives. We open our hearts to what You would do in Your time. Let us rest in Your time, Lord. Let us find peace in Your time. Let us share the story of Your time with others and one day, be caught up with You in timelessness. In Jesus Christ we pray. Amen.

My mommy-self is so thankful for His time. In it, things get done and people are grown, my heart is spread wide, and He fills it – with His hope, with Life, and with His peace.

I look forward to one more week of study with you all! It will be fun, as we wrap up our study of Ecclesiastes 3, with topics like vocation, eternity, and joy – all kinds of good stuff from His Word.

Exploration
What time of your life has felt the most hurried?

What time of your life do you feel sped by the fastest (in hindsight)? What time eked by the slowest?

What gifts of grace can you identify in God giving us the passing of time?

a conclusion to
ecclesiastes 3

Ecclesiastes 3:11a
He has made everything beautiful in its time.

week nine

A Conclusion
to Ecclesiastes 3

The great conundrum – Mama Life v. Work
On having it all...finding happy
Eternity in my heart and the "also-s" of faith
Time management v. time stewardship
Rising up from the dust

heart verse

For now we see in a mirror dimly, but then face to face. Now I know in part; then I shall know fully, even as I have been fully known.

1 Corinthians 13:12

a conclusion to ecclesiastes 3

day one
The great conundrum – Mama life v. Work

Wife, mother, daughter, sister, friend, pastor's wife, social worker, therapist… My many vocations, on this particular day, were getting the best of me. Where was the balance and how do other women magically find it?

One particular morning, as I kissed my children goodbye at school, one of them expressed great frustration and fear, targeted at life in general, but hitting me personally. "You just don't care anymore. You're always working. Work matters more to you."

My heart entered my stomach. I knew her words were fueled by the argument we had just abruptly ended, the chores no child wants to do, and the challenge of growing into independence. However, the question I asked myself, as a parent, was...Is there any truth in it? Even a morsel?

I found myself driving down the highway, struggling with what was most important in my life and how that propelled the way I spent my time each day. Was I casting aside my family, my children, my husband, those whom I love...for my work?

I wanted desperately to run back to the school and hash out this conversation with my beautiful daughter. I wanted to yell back, "I'm trying my best! I love you. I love my work. I love Jesus. I'm trying to mash them all together in a life that is going to be less than perfect."

I settled for crying in my parked van, waiting for the grocery store to open. In that moment, my distorted picture said to me in flashing marquee letters that I had failed...at everything...again.

After walking around Aldi, putting items in my cart and praying to God for forgiveness, I sat down at the coffee shop to work on Bible study. God is more clever than we give Him credit for. As I sat down, what was my previously outlined study concept for the day? Vocation. I love how He works like that – weaving pieces of His Word into the moments of our lives. His Word is surely living, breathing, and active.

The first text I opened to was Colossians 3:17. Read it with me. According to this text, what "work" is for the Lord, our God?

In your current season, are you generally content or frustrated with your duties? List below the ones you are easily contented with at present, and ones that currently bring you frustration. Be honest, there's no judgment here.

Content   Frustrated

What we do gives glory to Him. Some days, I find joy in the washing of the dishes, the packing of lunches, the parenting, the wife-ing, the cooking, as well as in the leading, the writing, and the teaching I do. Contentment in my callings comes and goes, as it does for most of us. On this day, in the grocery store parking lot, feeling like I was incapable of actually doing *any* of it to the best of my ability...that was my issue.

Sorting what to give time to each day, in a practical sense, is just plain hard. I know I'm not alone. I know many a wife and mom and worker feel paralyzed out there by a seeming inability to balance all the parts of life that work together – to find pleasure not in just the work, but in the knowledge that they have chosen *well* in their work on this earth.

Ecclesiastes to the rescue! Let's read Ecclesiastes 3:9-11.

I want gain from my toil. I want success and whatever that looks like in my worldly little mind. I want my children perfectly healthy and happy with me. I want my work to be excessively well done and reach and touch every single life around me. I want my husband to think I'm a rockstar. Ecclesiastes urges me to something different – to tone down my expectations.

The Lord wants me to do it well, but doing it well means simply doing it with an eternal perspective.

I am convinced that on this earth there will never be a moment where I find the perfect balance. There will be times that are more out of balance than others, and God can help me readjust, shift priorities around, but most of the time, "He has made everything beautiful in its time." One application of this statement means that this world will feel confusing, as I try to work within the element of time. There are many tasks to do, and the immediacy of the Gospel makes it feel like there is not enough time to do them. Friends, He has given us joy for our work, but not perfection. Perfection is for Him alone. He holds the time. He brings people to faith. He knows the day and hour.

Is it ok to settle for good instead of "success"? Yes! This is an important part of the doctrine of vocation to hash out. Write Colossians 3:17 below.

God doesn't say "Whatever you do, do it perfectly for the Lord, and in your amazing-ness they will see Jesus."

God has amazing under control. He doesn't need us to do that for Him, it wasn't ours to begin with. Just do it with your whole heart, for Him. It sounds so Ecclesiastes-ish. Do everything in Jesus' name. That is the fulfillment of vocation. My children see Jesus in me far better when I seek Him in all of it...in my uncertainty, in my insecurity, in my much-less-than-perfect, forgiveness-needing self. They see Him, when I pray with them after an argument, "God, help us figure all this out."

If I have learned anything from Ecclesiastes, it is this...

God makes everything beautiful, and most of the time, it takes time. It takes some amount of struggle. There is beauty in the figuring it out. Often, there is more beauty in the middle of figuring it out than in the solution. His Name is written all over my walk of figuring it out. His name is in the journey as much as in the eternal destination. He values the walking alongside.

Half of the struggle with my child is that we are still in the transition. I have only been doing this working mom thing for a short time, really, and we all need time to adjust, time to transition, time to talk it out. We won't ever get it perfect, but figuring it out together – I'm gonna call that very good.

Father, thank you for our families. Thank you for our work. Thank you for our homes, our fridges filled with food to cook, and our living rooms filled with things to pick up. Lord, help us to enjoy the journey in you. Help us to lay down everything before you. Guide and direct our days, let us eat the fruit of Your mercy and goodness in the joy of the everyday. Make all of our struggles beautiful in Your time. In Jesus' name, Amen.

Exploration
Go back to your list of your current vocations and duties. Pray over two of them and ask God to guide you in that work.

What aspects of your life do you have the hardest time balancing currently?

day two
On having it all and finding happy

It was in my late twenties that I learned the lesson of
happiness versus joy. Real joy, I mean. Joy spelled
J-E-S-U-S. That unchanging joy in the midst of struggle and
hardship. I remember learning this via an article I had found
and shared with the youth group. I'm not sure they got the
message, but it pierced me squarely in the heart. Maybe this
was a time in my life when I could most clearly hear it.
Maybe it had been spoken to me many times before and I
was only just then able to listen. Whatever the life-challenge
at the time, I began to look around me and hear with a fresh
heart the reality of a culture obsessed with happiness.
Do what makes you happy.
Go where you are happy.
Love the one who makes you happy.

These are the voices of a thousand commercials, the
endless rattle of the daytime talk shows, the lure of movies
and novels and a world that leaves us wanting. I started
studying Scripture unsatisfied with this and I found another
voice. Jesus tells us in His Word that He certainly wants us
to find Joy in Him and only Him. But don't be fooled – our
happiness matters to Him.

"What is this you say?! I have been like Solomon," you protest. "I have searched the world over. I have searched for happiness, I have worked for happiness. I have spent money to get happy. I have climbed the ladder to get happy, and I have learned that the world has little to offer, only Jesus brings the True to True Happiness."

Again, I would tell you that you are correct. However, if you read Ecclesiastes 3:11-14, I think you will find a better answer to the joy v. happiness battle. Let's read it.
 The God-breathed words of King Solomon in verse 12 tells us, *"I perceived that there is nothing better for them than to be joyful and to do good as long as they live..."*

Note the word choice here – *to be joyful*, not to have joy. The kind of joy recommended here is an action. The Hebrew word in the passage is *lismowah*. The word is from the root *samach*, which can mean a myriad of things from *rejoice, to make merry, to take pleasure in*, and yes, *to give happiness*.

The root word can be a subject, an adjective, but in every Biblical text this particular word, *lismowah*, is translated as a verb. With my limited Hebrew knowledge, this tells me that *lismowah* was meant to be an action. Most translations use a form of joy or rejoice, but the NIV is different. Read both the ESV and the NIV translations below. What difference do you see in the two translations?

> *I perceived that there is nothing better for them than to be joyful and to do good as long as they live...* (ESV)

> *I know that there is nothing better for people than to be happy and to do good while they live.* (NIV)

233

While we must take Ecclesiastes as a part within the whole of Scripture, we also cannot discount it. Psalm 106 also utilizes *lismowah*. Read Psalm 106:1-5 in any translation and print out verse 5 below. Circle the phrase that you think is translated from *lismowah*.

This psalm is a long song that tells the story of the generations of the Israelites turning from the Lord and ignoring His work, dishonoring Him. But it is also a psalm that proclaims the forgiveness, the pity, the mercy of the Lord to His people on earth. It is a psalm of unchanging joy, but it is also a psalm of the *experience* of that joy, and the overflowing happiness that is found in a life lived for the Lord. It tells the story of the Lord rushing to His people's aid. It gives praise to a Lord who physically and supernaturally fends off nations and keeps His people from destruction.

It is a psalm of the Lord giving happy for a certain time, along with joy unchanging.

The problem is not whether we should ask the Lord for joy over happiness. One is not diametrically opposed to the other. The problem comes in when we try to find happiness in things that are opposed to God. We will not find happy in tawdry television. We will not find happy in a man that sets God on a shelf. We will not find happy when we expect to find it in a big home with lots of things. Happiness in itself is not inherently evil. Happiness itself is a good gift of God, and we find it in oh-so-many things.

Happy looks a lot more like Jesus in our hearts, pouring out in a million different ways each day. Your context is different than mine. Where do you see your heart pouring over with happiness, as well as joy, to the world around you?

Happy isn't something you'll experience all the time. That isn't the goal. It's not what we were made for – happy, happy, and more happy. Sometimes, as Ecclesiastes is always quick to point out, our season is simply not happy. In those seasons of less than happy, we will still have Joy unchanging. While a particular season may not contain a whole lot of happy, other seasons will, in abundance!

Sit back, sister. Let the Spirit do His work. Ask Him to fill you with joy and to give you happiness, in its season. Take pleasure in the little things, even during a dark season, because you know they are provided by One who loves you infinitely and cares about even your happy.

Lord, I don't know the season each person is in. I ask You to pour out your mercies new every day, that you raise up Your Spirit to work in them in a new way, each day. Lord, thank You for the things that make us happy, for snowflakes and ice cream, for warm, sun-soaked skin and children laughing, for wine around a table of good friends, and a quiet moment spent alone. We praise You, Lord, that You give us Joy and You bring us happiness. Help us to always rejoice in the name of Your Son, Jesus. In His name, Amen.

Exploration

What people make you happy and why?

What things make you happy?

What are your thoughts on happiness and joy?

Share a prayer of rejoicing and praise for any of the things and people that God has given you in this season.

a conclusion to
ecclesiastes 3

day three
Eternity in my heart
and the "also-s" of faith

Also, He has put eternity into man's heart...
Ecclesiastes 3:11

What a beautiful phrase! Today we are going to break this tiny piece of Scripture into three intricate parts. It's just too beautiful not to spend some time on.

First, let's read a larger section of Scripture to get a fuller understanding. Feel free to read all of Ecclesiastes 3, or simply focus in on Ecclesiastes 3:11-13.

Let's work through the verses slowly.

First, the word *also*...
This small adverb sticks out to me. The Bible is a beautifully written Book, God-breathed, but also literarily lovely to behold. The words in the Bible are each there for a reason and the Old Testament especially holds so much poetic beauty. "Also" is a connecting word. God did such and such and *also* He has done this. "Also" is an overflowing-cup word (Psalm 23:5). The Hebrew word for *also* here is *gam*, in addition to being translated *also*, *gam* can be translated as *moreover*. Listen to that word – more and over, more than

that, over and above what our Savior has already done, overflowing our cups.

God takes things in our lives and makes them beautiful. Also, moreover, on top of that...He has given us eternity. He has set it in our hearts. What "also"s in life has God given you in this season? When you look around, what says to you, "My cup overflows..."? Share a few blessings the Lord has given to you in the space here.

Even if this is a difficult season, we all have something or someone, little things that give us glimpses of a God who is caring for us. It was in our darkest season that I began to recognize the "also"s, the little things that God gave in the form of people and tiny treasures of grace. These small also-s kept me going, and some days, they were what gave me the strength to get out of bed and face the challenge of a new day.

Next, He has put eternity in...
God gave us eternity as a free gift through Jesus Christ, our Lord and Savior. Ecclesiastes introduces an insight to consider. Eternity, in the broad sense, is for all people, not just believers of Christ Jesus. Everyone has an eternity. The question is where and how they will spend it. This insight is huge in relationship to the urgency of the Gospel and our compassion for those around us who do not know the grace of God.

God puts eternity into our hearts. Grace in Christ is a gift. Eternity, while certainly a gift, is a gift like our arms and legs and eyes – or even our heart – are gifts from God. We were created with eternity, set inside of us, by a loving God. It is part of who we are. It is meant to be a compass guiding us to Him. When people talk about the God-sized hole inside each of us, we can call that eternity. God wants us to embrace eternity with Him through Jesus Christ, but we can choose an eternity of darkness instead.

We are all searching, seeking, moving toward eternity. Many people simply do not have the language for what they are looking for. The next time you talk to an unbeliever, ask them what they are searching for, what they feel like they are heading toward in their life. When we are searching for a man to love us, the perfect job, parenting skills to keep our children on a good path, good memories, shared passions, ambitions fulfilled – all of it! – we are really looking for eternity. On top of just wanting those things and seeking, we all want it to matter, we want it to have significance, to know it was all worthwhile. As Christians, we have eternal life now. However, this also goes for the unbeliever sitting across from you. We all have eternity. They have significance that is eternal. Help lead them to the One their soul is searching for, that their internal compass is continuously trying to lead them to be in relationship with, rather than separated from. The darker side of this is that we are all accountable. There is life beyond this life on earth. Eternity with Him is incomparable to an eternity spent with the Evil One. How can I open this conversation to the person sitting across from me? The Lord knows. He has a plan. Take a moment to share the name of someone you'd like to share the message of eternity with.

Offer it up to our Heavenly Father in prayer. Ask Him to open the doors of conversation and connection with this person.

Last...he cannot find out what God has done from the beginning to the end.

We were not meant to know or understand it all. God does. If today's study feels like a bit much, and your mind is struggling to grasp it all, first, blame it on the author. I am an imperfect person talking about an absolutely perfect God; sometimes I have trouble spitting it all out in a manner that can be easily understood. Then, rest in this phrase: *We weren't meant to get it all. We were intended to seek Him, but not necessarily to always understand Him or what He is doing in our lives.* He is holier than that. He does not fit in our boxes, in our finite minds, even in our hearts. He is wider and bigger and outside of our thoughts and ways, even as He chooses each of us for His residence. Mind-blowing. That's our God.

What does 1 Corinthians 13:12 say about our understanding?

I return to this verse again and again. It's a good one for highlighting.

Now, read the very next verse, 1 Corinthians 13:13. What connection do you see between the two verses? How does one inform the other?

The greatest work God does in and through us is not knowledge, not even understanding, but love. He brought us to this place and this time to love; to love Him, to love His people, to love who He made us to be. When we look at our past, our present, and our eternity, we know that the only thing that will have mattered is that we were loved, and that we were given the chance to love Him in return. Eternity is set in our hearts.

Praise Him today for His love, His the eternity He gives us, and His overflowing abundance.

Exploration
What things or people in your life currently remind you that your cup overflows?

When has fixing your eyes on eternity been most helpful for you?

What do you see people searching for, when they are really searching for God?

a conclusion to
ecclesiastes 3

day four
Time stewardship v. time management

Sometimes life can seem completely and utterly chaotic. We have ventured into my problem with time before in this Bible study. The more I attempt to be on time or really to control time, to manage time, the more I am likely to show up late, spiral into the abyss of anxiety, and trample over someone I didn't intend to hurt. I'm not suggesting that organization is a negative thing. I am suggesting that the more we try to control, the more God will begin to show us that we are very much not in control.

My husband and I embraced a new concept for our lives – time stewardship. Living in the realm of time management never quite fit for either of us. It sounds like a small change, but trading in management for stewardship, recognizing that time belonged to the Lord and not to us, helped us to put our priorities in the right place, as well as to slow down and enjoy the journey. It lifted the burden of guilt when we chose to sit instead of work, when we said no to something that took time away from the family, or when we entered a busy season and we had to pick tighter boundaries than normal.

Time is a funny thing. I think it challenges us to remember our place within God's universe. It forces us to see who God is and how small we really are. So what happens? Most people choose to ignore it as a concept. We fill our lives with

242

busyness, with appointments, with fun, with entertainment, with rest, with work, with friendships...whatever will keep us from thinking about the clock that has been set in each one of us. "Time waits for no man" as the saying goes. The clock keeps ticking, with or without us.

Time, above all else, means change. Seconds turn into minutes, minutes turn into hours, hours into days, and years, and lifetimes. It will not be held in our tight fist. Change reminds us that we are not in control. Please read Ecclesiastes 3:14-15, where we are reminded that only God lasts forever. What words in the passage remind you that we are small compared to our Great God?

Whatever God does, whatever He touches, endures forever. Whatever we do without Him passes away. We have nothing new to add.

The good news about our smallness is... God can hold us.

When the verse tells us "God has done it", one thing we can be assured of is that He created time for us, not for Himself. This gift is that exact reminder that left us shaking in our boots when we realized how small we are. When things change, and time marches on, we stand in the arms of a God who is big. To fear God is to recognize that He is capable. To know Him is to know that He is trustworthy. He is unshakable. When the whole world seems to be changing faster than we can keep up, He does not change.

"God seeks that which is driven away" or more literally, "God seeks that which is pursued." This part of the passage was so confusing for me, so difficult to understand, that I made a chart for myself on a post it note and convinced my husband to hash it out with me. After studying and rooting around Scripture, this is where we landed: God is a pursuer. He loves us so much that He pursues us on a timeline which is our life.

I'm writing this during Lent and I keep coming back to the faces of the disciples who were left in confusion after Jesus died and rose. They went back to time as they understood it. They went back to their meeting place in the upper room, to their boats to fish. They didn't understand the life-changing events of Holy Week, *but God sought them.* He walked out of the tomb and appeared to them in the upper room. He found them on the shore as they cast out their nets. *God sought them and He seeks us.* This doesn't change with the time or the season or the ticking of the clock as the hands move on by.

Psalm 136 is the perfect ending for today's abstract study. Read it aloud, if you feel comfortable. Note what reminders you find in the psalm that relate to time and God's greatness.

God's love is the same yesterday, today, and forever. He's got the whole world in His hands. He knows the day and the hour. His steadfast love surely endures forever.

Exploration
How does eternity change life now for both the believer and the unbeliever?

What changes in life have you resisted from God before?

Recite Psalm 136 responsively with your husband, your family, or a friend. Share together what insights you find about God within it.

a conclusion to
ecclesiastes 3

day five
Rising up from the dust

When I was a sophomore in high school my parents took me out of class to go to the 10AM Ash Wednesday service at church. I can't remember the reason, but something prohibited us from going in the evening and this was how my parents rolled.

I came back to school about lunchtime, completely unaware of the cross blazed across my forehead. Twenty minutes later, one of my male classmates, who shall remain nameless, walked up to me and stammered, "What's on your face?" and proceeded to rub my head vigorously to remove the cross.

I stood in shock, all systems shut down from the basic humiliation. I turned on my heel, walked to the bathroom, entered a stall, and promptly burst into tears. I didn't know what to think. I didn't really know why I was upset. I did know that something about his actions rocked me deep to my core.

I said a silent prayer, gathered myself, and walked out of the bathroom stall, directly to the unnamed classmate and said quietly, "You may not touch my personhood again. You may not defame what I hold dear. His name is Jesus and you should probably get to know Him."

This, friends, was a Holy Spirit moment in my life, if there ever was one. These words were not my own, they tumbled out and into the situation of their own free will. How do I know this?

Here's a little of my story. In my youth, I dutifully followed the religion of my parents, I embraced Lutheranism head on, not because I believed it at that point, but because I needed it to reign me in. Sophomore year was the worst and my moral compass was all over the place, laced with feminism, hedonism, and many other -isms thrown in for good measure. I knew Jesus because He called me in my baptism, but I didn't trust Him enough to include Him in my life and I surely, at this point, wasn't introducing anyone else to Him.

Ecclesiastes 3:20 gives us some Biblical perspective on Ash Wednesday ashes –

> All go to the same place; all come from dust, and to dust all return.

Dust and ashes on my forehead were what woke me up from a youthful spiritual stupor. I started searching for Jesus with everything I had, to find out that He had found me long ago, and my heart was filled to the brim with just how shockingly deep the Father's love for each of us truly is.

247

Dust isn't our whole story, but it certainly is a huge component of it. What insight does each of the following passages in Ecclesiastes give us for where we come from and where we are going?

Ecclesiastes 3:19-21

Ecclesiastes 12:1-7

I'm sure the writer of Ecclesiastes was just as wowed by God's full plan when He saw Jesus' face in heaven, as we are when we read it in His Word. Let's take a minute to be wowed, friends. Let's follow the trail of God's dust from creation to purposeful destruction, to resurrection and on to restoration.

Everything is beautiful in its time. This is what our study, if anything, has taught us.

Starting at the beginning, Creation...
Please read Genesis 2:5-7. We were formed from what substance?

By whom were we formed?

How did He form us?

I wonder at the conversation between the persons of the Trinity at this moment of creation.

Purposeful Destruction...
Read Genesis 3:17-19 and see a primary example of when destruction is purposeful.

> And to Adam he said,
>> "Because you have listened to the voice of your wife
>>> and have eaten of the tree
>> of which I commanded you,
>>> 'You shall not eat of it,'
>> cursed is the ground because of you;
>>> in pain you shall eat of it all the days of your life;
>> thorns and thistles it shall bring forth for you;
>>> and you shall eat the plants of the field.
>> By the sweat of your face
>>> you shall eat bread,
>> till you return to the ground,
>>> for out of it you were taken;
>> for you are dust,
>>> and to dust you shall return."

Underline or circle every reference to the ground or dust in the verses above.

Sin brought destruction to our world, but God would use it for His purposes. He would create a space that would allow in discipline and trial to show us His grace through it. Even this, He will make beautiful.

You could also look at the Babylonian captivity to see God's work in purposeful destruction – of His temple, of His people, of the way people thought it would be...all to lead us to Him. Flip to Isaiah 17 or Daniel 9. Share what kind of destruction you find in one of these passages.

What good came from the destruction?

God is always leading us back to Him through the destruction.

Christ walks in the dust...
Look up two or three of the following verses, or all of them if you're feeling bold! Write next to the reference what relationship Christ had to dust or dirt in the passage.

Luke 2:6-7

Psalm 113:7

John 8:1-11

Matthew 26:38-39

John 19:41-42

Christ is born among the dust of animal feed. He bends down into the dust to lift up weary souls burdened with the weight of sin, oppression, and judgement during His time on earth. He let His face be ground into the dust as He took our sins on Himself and bore our iniquities. And He was eventually laid in a dusty tomb, carved out of the rock.

Christ is risen from the dust...
Let's read this account, even if we've heard it a hundred times – Matthew 28:1-7 –

Verse 6 proclaims beauty from the ashes,
beauty out of the dust...

> *He is not here, for he has risen, as he said.*
> *Come, see the place where he lay.*

See where he lay. He's not there. He did what He said.
Thank you, Jesus.

Restoration from the dust...
Whether we're talking about personal restoration or the restoration of the whole of creation, Jesus is surely faithful.

What do each of these passages tell us are received from dust and ashes?

Isaiah 61:1-3

Acts 3:18-21

Write Acts 3:21 here:

Restoration...everything beautiful in its time. In His time.

What does this mean for you? What has Jesus restored or what are you waiting for Him to restore in your life?

How do you think creation will look different in the Restoration, when Christ comes again?

The Last Day isn't just about judgement and terror. For Christians, it's about the culmination of time, everything being eagerly restored by a God we know intimately, time reaching the pentacle of all things. Praise be to Him!

That day in high school years ago, I had no idea why my forehead dust meant so much. Now, when I go to Him in prayer and worship, when my pastor places the ashes on my forehead and proclaims, "From dust you came, From dust you shall arise!" I know. On Easter morning, when I heartily reply, "He is Risen indeed! Alleluia!", I praise Him for using moments of humiliation, moments of destruction, moments of struggle, moments of joy, moments of peace, moments of confusion, moments of understanding.

Everything beautiful in His time. Every moment, all things worthwhile found in Him.

Thank you for taking the last nine weeks to study with me. I have learned and been stretched, and I pray you have been, too.

Until next time, In Him, much love,
Heidi ♡

References

It is Well -
http://hymnary.org/text/when_peace_like_a_river_attendeth_my_way

Matthew Henry's Commentary - Bible Gateway - March 2016
Retrieved from
https://www.biblegateway.com/resources/matthew-
henry/Eccl.3.1-Eccl.3.22

Muth. From *Strong's Hebrew.* Retrieved from
http://biblehub.com/hebrew/strongs_4191.htm

Pelikan, J. (Ed.). (1972). *Luther's Works, Vol. 15:
Ecclesiastes, Song of Solomon, and the Last Words of
David.* St. Louis, MO: Concordia Publishing House.

We Gather Together -
http://www.hymnary.org/text/we_gather_together_to_ask_th
e_lords

Thank you for studying the Word with me! If you have any thoughts, questions, or would like permission to copy a portion of this book, please contact the author, Deaconess Heidi Goehmann, MSW, LISW at hlgoehmann@gmail.com or ilovemyshepherd.com. I would love to hear from you!

I am deeply grateful to my family, friends, colleagues, and readers for their encouragement and support, particularly: Sarah Baughman, editor extraordinaire and ever thoughtful friend. Thank God He saw fit to bring you into my life! Dave, Macee, Jonah, Jyeva, and Zeke for all the sacrifices of time, energy, and sanity you make for me to do ministry. Melissa Ripke, whose graphic designs are always gorgeous, fresh, and hope-filled. Our Ohio church and community – you saw us through the darkness by shining His Light brighter than I ever thought possible. You cannot know the difference and the indelible mark you have made on our hearts and lives.

Made in the USA
Coppell, TX
22 March 2021